a short history of
⌐cape cod⌐

a short history of

cape cod

Robert J. Allison

COMMONWEALTH EDITIONS
BEVERLY, MASSSACHUSETTS

For Evelyn and Phil Gaudiano
Two Cape Codders—
One by birth, one by choice

Library of Congress Cataloging-in-Publication Data
Allison, Robert J.
    A short history of Cape Cod / Robert J. Allison.
    p. cm.
Includes bibliographical references.
ISBN 978-1-889833-99-6 (alk. paper)
1. Cape Cod (Mass.)—History. 2. Cape Cod (Mass.)—History—Pictorial works. 3. Cape Cod (Mass.)— Biography. I. Title.

F72.C3A655 2010
974.4'92—dc22   2009043394

Front cover image: William Allen Wall, *Gosnold at Smoking Rocks:* Bartholomew Gosnold and his men trade and celebrate with Native people. (Courtesy New Bedford Whaling Museum)

Printed in the USA

Series design by Laura McFadden Design, Inc.

Published by Commonwealth Editions, an imprint of Memoirs Unlimited, Inc., 266 Cabot Street, Beverly, MA 01915, www.commonwealtheditions.com

10 9 8 7 6 5 4 3 2 1

The artist Alice Stallknecht painted her neighbors in front of Chatham's Methodist Church. (Chatham Historical Society)

Ross Moffett, *Shankpainter Pond,* 1925. Ice was necessary to keep fish cold; Moffett painted the ice cutters on one of Provincetown's ponds. (Collection of the Town of Provincetown, courtesy Provincetown Art Commission)

contents

A bird's-eye view of Provincetown, with the Cape's tip in the lower left, and in the distance the Plymouth horizon. (Courtesy: Historic New England)

view from Long Point

FROM THE END OF LONG POINT, you can see ten thousand years of history.

The Native people called the Cape's tip Meeshawn, "where there is going by boat." Stand here and you are surrounded by water, though the water is bound all around by land. Your eye can follow the curve of land west to Wood End, north to the shore of Provincetown, east to the Pamet River and the highlands of Truro, and then south again to the cliffs of Wellfleet. The land vanishes from sight southeast across Cape

Cod Bay, where off in the distance lie Barnstable and Sandwich and the canal.

Whales still feed offshore, and seals still surface, and diving birds reveal underwater schools of fish. Wind and tide have shaped the land much more than the men and women who have lived on this narrow stretch of sand. Native men and women built their canoes from the great trees that once grew here, caught whales, and gathered fish along the shore. Thorwald the Viking may have repaired his ship in this great harbor, which Bartholomew Gosnold wanted to call Shoal

The Cape's oldest windmill, in Yarmouth; it has since been moved to Michigan.

Hope, or "shallow harbor." His men pointed to the fish teeming below the surface and told him to call the place Cape Cod.

Eighteen years after Gosnold's brief stay, the *Mayflower* brought the Pilgrims to this harbor. They agreed to be governed by laws they themselves would make. The British warship *Somerset* sailed into this harbor in the 1770s, trying to impose authority on their descendants who took this notion of self-government too far.

By the early nineteenth century the nation had become independent, the trees were gone, and the Pilgrim descendants had bought the land from the Native people. They built saltworks on the sandy beaches and windmills to harvest the one resource they could not exhaust. They built lighthouses: Long Point on the tip, and off to the south and east on the highlands of Truro is Cape Cod or Highland Light, warning mariners of the deadly bars off the outer beach. The mariners, descendants of Yankees or immigrants from the Azores or Cape Verde, ventured out after cod, tuna, and whales. John Kendrick took ships to the Pacific in the 1780s, opening American trade with China; one hun-

Provincetown looking like a typical New England village in the 1920s. (Provincetown Art Commission)

dred years later, in the 1880s, Lorenzo Dow Baker of Wellfleet brought lumber from South America and Jamaica; he also brought back bananas and dreams of luxury hotels.

Theodore Roosevelt sailed into this harbor to lay the Pilgrim Monument cornerstone in 1907, and three years later his stout successor, Taft, came to dedicate it. The Atlantic fleet was here during the First and Second World Wars; in 1917 a nervous government shut down the radio towers Gugliemo Marconi had built in Wellfleet, and the following year German submarines came close enough to shell Orleans. During the years after the war the U.S. Navy experimented here with submarines; the S-4 went down off Wood End in 1927, rammed by a Coast Guard boat.

During the tense war years a vigilant townsperson reported a suspected spy in the dunes; he turned out to be Eugene O'Neill, seeking to put into dramatic form the interior tragedies of the new century. After learning he had won the Pulitzer Prize, he took a celebratory plunge into the cold Atlantic. Whereas O'Neill and others wrote, trying to put into words the world they knew, Charles Hawthorne and Blanche Lazzell tried to capture the world in images of oil and ink, creating an American art with the light of the outer Cape.

Today the harbor is tranquil, but it has seen turmoil and tragedy. Men once set out to hunt whales from this harbor, but today boats go to watch the whales and study them. The land remains, though it continues to

Warships in Provincetown Harbor, 1918. (Historic New England)

Provincetown's West End Beach. (Historic New England)

change, as the relentless tide and wind reshape it and remove all evidence that any of us—Natives or Vikings, Pilgrims or presidents, explorers, warriors, poets, painters, or entrepreneurs—ever set foot on this sandy beach. ⌒

1

gosnold's hope

SCIENTISTS TELL US THAT glaciers pushed up this ridge of sand to create Cape Cod, then dropped chunks of ice into it to form kettle ponds. The Native people who lived here before the scientists arrived had their own explanations, which unfortunately they did not write down.

The Native women planted corn, squash, beans, and tobacco beneath the great trees. The men made the trees into canoes, long and wide enough to carry a dozen men. Every spring they gathered the herring that ran up the streams, and in the ponds—350 ponds, more than seventeen square miles of fresh water—they caught eels and turtles. On the flats left by the retreating tides they dug quahogs and oysters; at the rocky places they found mussels. They could harpoon whales and dolphins that strayed too close to shore. They dried the fish and meat, pounding them together with the tart red cranberries from the bogs.

They housed themselves in wigwams, or *wetus,* of bark and deer-skins, and they dressed in the skins of deer and seals. In winter they buried their baskets of corn deep in the sand. For more complicated exchanges they wove strands of wampum, beads made from the qua-hogs' purplish shells and the mussels' black shells.

Each Cape band, from Succonesset and Manomet to Nauset and Meeshawn, was independent and autonomous. Each village might be friendly or not with its neighbors. Each village had a sachem chosen to lead, but not to rule. Their language—part of the Algonquian fam-ily—and ways of life were similar to those of native people from east-ern Canada to Virginia. They were loosely allied with the Wampanoags, or "Eastern People," who lived between the eastern shores of Narragansett Bay and the Massachusetts coast at Duxbury.

If one envisions the Cape as an arm, Manomet was at the shoulder. South along Buzzards Bay was Succonesset, or "black shells," the mus-sels found "where the waters open out," or in the Native language, Poughkeeste. The south coast traverses Cotuit and Massipee, "the

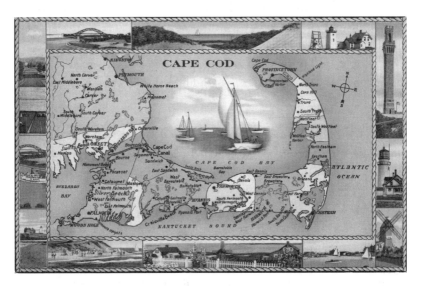

A map of Cape Cod. (Courtesy Historic New England)

great water." Monomoy, at the elbow, is the "rushing of mighty waters." The north coast, along Cape Cod Bay, takes the traveler through Cummaquid, or "the other side of the water," and the "old fields" of Mattacheese, through the "tidal river outlet" of Saquatucket to Namskaket, "the place for harvesting little fish."

Nauset, "the place between," stretches north from Monomoy between the Atlantic and the calmer waters of Cape Cod Bay. The land narrows farther north, where the winters are more severe. At Chequessett, "the large land place" and Pamet, the little stream "at the sea," villagers lived off their oyster beds and the whales that ventured too close to shore. Finally, at Meeshawn, "where there is going by boat," the sandy finger curls around the world's second largest natural harbor.

An arriving visitor would be taken to the sachem. No one would speak. Instead, all would smoke a pipe of tobacco. When they finished smoking, the sachem would ask, "Whence do you come?" After hearing an answer, the sachem would announce whether the stranger could stay or must leave. If the people agreed, they would assent by saying, "He." If not, they would remain silent, then one by one tell the sachem their opinion. When all had spoken, the sachem would explain the decision to the guest.

Visitors had been coming for many years. After 1600 more visitors began to arrive. Most came to trade. This did not change the lives of the people, who had always traded. Others came to fish, but the people of the narrow land had always fished. But then more came to take away people, and others to take land. These arrivals forever changed the life the people of the narrow land had always known.

Bartholomew Gosnold and thirty-two men left Falmouth, England, on the ship *Concord* in March 1602. Gosnold hoped to begin a New World colony. By May they were off Newfoundland; when he reached the coast of Maine three men rowed in a small boat out from the rocky shore. Two wore European clothes—waistcoat, shoes, and stockings, one in black serge pants, the other in blue cloth breeches—the other wore deer- and sealskins. These men "seemed to understand more than we . . . could comprehend," and drew a map on a rock. They invited Gosnold to stay, but their map told him he was too far north. The *Concord* sailed south across the open water.

The next day, Saturday, May 15, the voyagers spied land, highlands that seemed to rise out of the water. Sailing west around this apparent island, Gosnold brought the *Concord* to anchor in a broad harbor. Gosnold called it "Shoal Hope," or shallow harbor. We call it Provincetown. Gosnold and four men rowed to the "white sandy and very bold shore." Shouldering their muskets, they walked into the hills. They found unripe peas and strawberries. From the highest hills they saw that this was no island. It was a cape arching back to the mainland, twenty miles to the west.

Back on the beach they met a young man "of proper stature and of a pleasing countenance," carrying a bow and arrow, copper plates dangling from his ears. "He showed a willingness to help us in our occasions," the sailor Gabriel Archer recalled. The men who stayed on the *Concord* spent the day catching "great stores of codfish," so many that when Captain Gosnold returned they told him this place should be called Cape Cod.

Cape Cod it became. For many years Cape Cod referred only to the broad harbor and the land surrounding it. But by the nineteenth century Cape Cod was all of the narrow land stretching back to Manomet.

Gosnold sailed out of the harbor and around Race Point, then south along thirty-six miles of unbroken shore. The party then found the breach that the natives called Monomoyick for its mighty rushing waters. Gosnold called it Point Care. Westward they sailed. Just past Gilbert's Point, now the entrance to Hyannis Harbor, more Indians paddled out to trade.

All wore copper pendants from their ears, and one had a copper breastplate a foot long and half a foot wide. These men were "more timorous than those of Savage Rock," in Maine, "yet very thievish." Crossing the sound, the *Concord* on May 22 reached the island of Aquinnah, or Capewock. The strawberries and raspberries were abundant, and the grapevines seemed to run up every tree. Gosnold called it a vineyard, and named it for his infant daughter back home: Martha's Vineyard. The men caught codfish, "as before at Cape Cod, but much better." Thirteen Natives decked out in copper approached "unto us in great familiarity" with tobacco, hides, and fish.

Sailing north and west, they landed again and "stood awhile," wrote John Brereton, who was one of those aboard, "like men ravished at the beauty and delicacy of this sweet soil." Compared to this rich land, Brereton wrote, "the most fertile part of all England is (of itself) but barren." On May 24 they entered "one of the stateliest sounds" that Gabriel Archer, who wrote another account of the voyage, had ever seen. The Indians called it Poughkeeste. Gosnold called it Gosnold's Hope. Across it lay "the goodliest continent that we ever saw," Archer wrote, "promising more by far than we any did expect."

"Notwithstanding our diet and lodging," which were poor, the climate itself was so wholesome "we found our health & strength all the while we remained there, so to renew and increase." Only one man took sick, and that was because he ate too many of the "very delicious" dogfish bellies. The men all "were much fatter and in better health than when we went out of England." Archer wrote of the Cape's "fair fields," filled with "fragrant flowers, also meadows, and hedged in with stately groves," the "pleasant brooks" and the beautiful "two main rivers that . . . may haply become good harbors, and conduct us to the hopes men so greedily do thirst after."

Gosnold made his colony on an island the Natives called Cuttyhunk. Natives did not live on Cuttyhunk but went there to harvest crabs. According to a story the Indians told, the Devil had been building a stone bridge to these islands when a crab caught his finger. The Devil flung the crab to the distant islands, where crabs continue to breed. Gosnold named the island Elizabeth, after either his wife or his queen. The name did not stick; it remained Cuttyhunk, the last link in the chain still named for Elizabeth, Gosnold or Tudor.

In a huge pond on Cuttyhunk Island there is an island an acre in size. Gosnold and his men chose this island on an island for their settlement. He planned to stay with twenty men, sending the others home with a cargo of cedar, furs, and sassafras, thought to cure everything from kidney stones to syphilis.

Eleven canoes appeared on June 5, carrying fifty "stout and lusty men with their bows and arrows." Brereton and eight men were on their island, Gosnold and the rest of the English on the *Concord*. Brereton clapped his hands to his head and chest, then presented his gun: the choice was peace or war. The native leader understood, "using me with mine own signs of peace," and Brereton stepped forward to embrace him. The Indians sat back on their heels, in a way that always intrigued the English.

Gosnold and twelve men arrived from the ship. Brereton had the shore party form an honor guard for Gosnold, signaling to the Indians that he was their captain. Gosnold presented the Indian leader with a straw hat and a pair of knives, "and this our courtesy made them all in love with us." The Indians left in friendship. Two days later they came back for lunch. They enjoyed the Englishmen's codfish and beer, though they "made many a sour face" at mustard. No one made sour faces at the crabs and herring the Indians caught and roasted, and all afternoon the men ate, smoked, and traded furs.

There was one tense moment when one of the Indians tried to stash an English target on a canoe. Both the English and the Indians reprimanded him, the target was returned, and the smoking and eating and trading continued until the leader rose to leave. Four Indians stayed behind to help the English gather sassafras. This Cuttyhunk beach party gave Gosnold great hope for the success of his colony.

One Indian man brought his wife and daughter to see the English. They were the first Englishmen the women had ever seen, and the women were the first these men had seen since March. The women were "clean and straight-bodied," their countenances "sweet and pleasant," though the Indian man "gave heedful attendance" to them as they showed "much familiarity with our men, although they would not admit of any immodest touch."

Gosnold had great hope for his colony in this fertile land. Within two weeks English seeds his men had planted were half a foot high. But as the men finished the stronghouse and loaded the *Concord* with sassafras, lumber, and furs, they had second thoughts. Only twelve now were willing to stay. Gosnold did not think twelve men could sustain the colony. So on June 18, 1602, "with as many true sorrowful eyes, as were before desirous to see it," Gosnold and his men sailed for England.

None would return to Cape Cod. Gosnold did not give up his dream of a New World colony. In 1606 the London Company hired him to help plant a colony on the Chesapeake. Gosnold went to Virginia, but he did not believe Jamestown was a wise site for the settlement. He was right. He died of malaria in 1607.

But Gosnold's stories of this fertile land and its cod-filled waters spread. Others came, lacking Gosnold's personality and ability to get along with those he met. Captain George Weymouth visited in

1605, and he kidnapped five Cape Cod and Vineyard Indians to take home as souvenirs. Ferdinando Gorges, a promoter of New World investments, took in three of the Indians to show off to colonial investors.

One of these Indians, Epenow, told Gorges that Martha's Vineyard was rich in gold. He would lead them to it if they took him back. His ruse worked. Though the English guarded him closely, he told them he would need to dress in native clothing to earn his countrymen's trust. As Indians in their canoes surrounded the ship, the nearly naked Epenow walked onto the bowsprit. In a sudden shower of arrows he dove into the water. The English thought their faithful translator had been killed in the attack and withdrew. They lost Epenow, but not the hope of finding gold on Martha's Vineyard.

The English were not the only ones interested in the New World. A group of French in 1605 came south from their base at Port Royal, in what is now Nova Scotia, hoping to find a more pleasant place to spend the winter. They stayed a week at Nauset Harbor, finding the Nauset people friendly. But this changed quickly when the French accused a Nauset of stealing an iron kettle. In the ensuing fight one Frenchman was killed and one Indian was

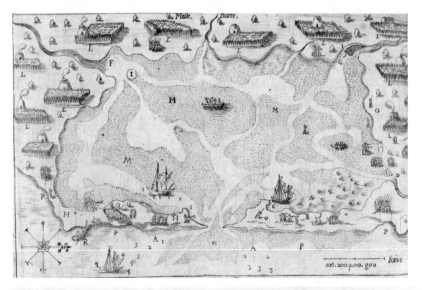

Nauset Harbor, with its large Indian villages, as it appeared to Champlain in 1606. (Courtesy John Carter Brown Library, Brown University, Providence, R.I.)

Samuel Champlain sketched the harbor of Monomoy, and the large Indian villages around it, after his 1606 visit. (Courtesy John Carter Brown Library, Brown University, Providence, R.I.)

taken prisoner. The French released him and left Nauset Harbor, naming it Port Mallebare.

After another winter in Port Royal, Jean de Poutrincourt led a second expedition to Cape Cod. Among his party were Samuel de Champlain and Secondon, leader of the St. John's River Indians. Their reunion with the Nausets in October 1606 was more amicable than their departure had been. They continued on, past Monomoy, trying to put in as they saw columns of smoke rising from the villages onshore. The outer beach's surf nearly swamped their boat. The Monomoy launched a canoe, advising the French to sail farther south and round Monomoy Point.

Were the Indians being helpful? The breakers grew more intense as they sailed south, smashing their rudder. Scraping along in the dangerously shallow water—twelve feet, nine feet, six feet, three feet— "by the grace of God" they rounded the point. Poutrincourt brought the ship to anchor outside Stage Harbor. An Englishman, Daniel Hay, was sent to determine whether the harbor was safe. A Monomoy greeted him, signaling safety. Hay brought him back to the ship, hoping Secondon could talk with him, but neither could understand the other. The Monomoys guided the crippled ship into the harbor.

The French arrived in October; Gosnold had passed through in May. These may be the Cape's best months. The French found abundant wild grapes, hickory nuts, and beach plums, and the Indians' corn was ripe. "All the harbors, bays, and coasts are filled with every variety of fish," including shellfish, Champlain wrote. He was particularly impressed with the oysters.

Oddly enough for a coastal expedition, the French brought no fishing equipment. They did bring guns. "Game birds are very plenty," Champlain observed, and Poutrincourt reportedly killed twenty-eight "sea larks" with one shot.

If only Monomoy had a better harbor, Champlain thought, it would make an excellent capital for New France. Five or six hundred people already lived here, "their bodies well proportioned and their skin olive-colored. They adorn themselves with feathers, beads of shells and other gewgaws, which they arrange very neatly in embroidery work." Not great hunters, the Monomoys were fishermen and farmers. Champlain noted that they planted corn and beans together; the growing corn stalk supported the bean vine.

But the French and the Monomoys clashed. A Frenchman accused an Indian of stealing an axe; the Indians fled as the French fired after them. The French feared an attack when the Monomoys took down their wigwams and their women and children moved into the woods. The French bought peace by giving the women bracelets and rings, the elders hatchets and knives. Champlain does not explain why, if they suspected the Indians "wished to play some bad trick," they gave them hatchets and knives. The elders and the women then did "dances, gambols, and harangues" that the French did not understand.

Poutrincourt marked the territory with a cross, then ordered all his men back onto the ship. Bakers stayed behind to finish their loaves, along with two men hoping to eat fresh cakes. Early the next morning four hundred Indians descended on the five sleeping Frenchmen, sending "such a volley of arrows that to rise up was death." The men on the ship said the "roarings" of the attackers were "terrible to hear" as the besieged bakers cried, "Help! They are killing us!" Two men were already dead in the water, and two others pierced with arrows when the rescue party set out. Low tide made it impossible to get close to shore, so the rescuers jumped into the water and chased the Monomoys into the woods.

Under Poutrincourt's cross the French buried their two dead comrades, chanting prayers and firing the ship's cannon as the Monomoys howled derisively from the woods. Once the French left the shore, the Monomoys tore down the cross, dug up the dead, and prepared to burn them. More French went ashore, and the Monomoys again vanished. The French raised their cross and reburied their dead, but once they were on the ship the Monomoys tore down the cross and opened the grave.

The French sailed the next day, naming this place of misfortune Port Fortune. They sailed west. Some of the men spied Martha's Vineyard, but their superiors doubted it and called what they saw *La Soupçonneuse*, the doubtful. When they reached the area that is now Falmouth, they avenged themselves on the Monomoys by kidnapping Indians. The French showed the Indians "beads and other gewgaws, and assure[d] them repeatedly of our good faith." When an Indian came close enough the French wrapped the beads around his neck and bound his arms and chest. Indians who resisted too strenuously were killed.

The Indians did resist. None would be taken alive, but the French killed and cut off the heads of seven. As the French sailed back along the coast, the mobilized Indians tried to lure them to shore, but the French sailed straight back to Port Royal. After another Canadian winter, they returned to France.

Over the next decade, European explorers passed by, trading with or kidnapping the Natives. None stayed. Henry Hudson on the Dutch ship *Half Moon* stopped at the Cape's tip in April 1609, noting the grape and rose plants and Natives. He sailed on to what would be named the Hudson River. Edward Harlow came from England's Isle of Wight, searching for gold on Martha's Vineyard. He did not find it, but he did kidnap three Indians from the Cape—Peckmo, Monopet, and Pekenimme—and three from Martha's Vineyard and Nantucket. Peckmo escaped. He and friends returned to the ship and stole Harlow's boat. English accounts focus on Peckmo's theft, not Harlow's. The nineteenth-century historian Charles Francis Adams wrote that "history has recorded not much" the Indians' "side of the story. Saying little of their wrongs, it dwells at length on their treachery, their cruelty, and their extermination."

John Smith had gone with Gosnold to Jamestown in 1607. Like Gosnold, Smith recognized Virginia's sickliness, and he heard from Gosnold about the healthier and more fertile Cape. After the Jamestown colonists expelled Smith, he made a voyage to map this region east of the Hudson River. This area—stretching from New Amsterdam to New France—Smith named New England.

Smith described Cape Cod as being "in the form of a sickle; on it doth inhabit the people of Pawmet; and in the bottom of the Bay the people of Chawrum." He did not see but described the "long and dangerous shoal of sands and rocks" south of the Cape. He described the Cape's tip as "only a headland of high hills of sand overgrown with shrubby pines, hurts [i.e., whortleberries or blueberries], and such trash, but an excellent harbor for all weathers."

Smith left Captain Thomas Hunt behind in New England, catching cod for the Spanish market. Hunt caught more than cod. He kidnapped twenty men from Patuxet (now Plymouth) and seven from Nauset, and he sold each in Malaga, Spain, for twenty pounds.

Shortly after Hunt left, a French fishing boat wrecked on the Cape. The crew made it to shore, but the Native people saw an opportunity to avenge themselves for Hunt's evil. They killed all but five of the French and traded these five as slaves to people as far away as Namasket, now Middleborough, and Massachuseck, now the Boston area. One of the Frenchmen married a Native woman and fathered her child.

Meanwhile, in Malaga a Spanish monk freed the Indians whom Hunt had kidnapped. One of them, Tisquantum (also called Squanto), from Patuxet, made it back to Newfoundland, where he met Captain Thomas Dermer, who had been sent to find the elusive gold of Martha's Vineyard. Dermer thought Tisquantum would be useful in this mission and took him along.

Much had changed since Tisquantum had been kidnapped. A mysterious plague had devastated the Massachusetts coastal communities, killing up to 90 percent of the people and wiping out entire villages, including Tisquantum's Patuxet. Dermer "passed alongst the Coast where I found some ancient Plantations, not long since populous but now void; in other places a remnant remains, but not free of sickness."

When they reached Patuxet, "finding all dead," Dermer sent a messenger forty miles west to Pokanoket, now Bristol, Rhode Island.

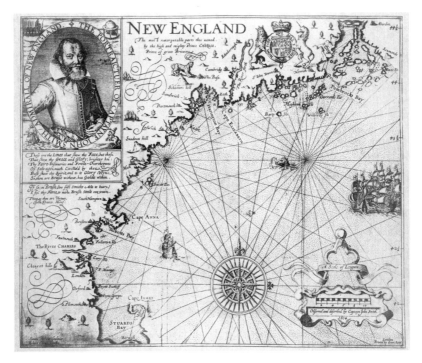

John Smith's 1614 map of the New England coast inspired the Pilgrims. (Courtesy Massachusetts Historical Society)

Back came two Indian leaders—possibly the sachem Massassoit and his brother—accompanied by fifty men. After brief discussions, "being well satisfied with what my savage and I discoursed unto them," Dermer's men were allowed to explore, and Massassoit turned over one of the French captives. Dermer selected seven places to dig for gold, and leaving Tisquantum at Sawahquatooke, near today's Brewster, he sailed on, rounding the Cape.

A sudden storm threatened to destroy his craft, which the men saved only by throwing all their provisions overboard. Dermer went ashore at Monomoy but was immediately taken captive. He promised a ransom in hatchets (all he had to offer). When the sachem went aboard to collect, Dermer's men raised anchor and set sail. The sachem "would have leaped overboard," begging Dermer's pardon and returning the hatchets. The sachem dispatched a man to bring Dermer a canoe-load of corn.

After this narrow escape at Monomoy, Dermer sailed for Martha's Vineyard, where he was astonished to meet Epenow, who "was report-

The Gosnold Monument, on Gosnold Island. (Photo by Hal Granger; courtesy Elizabeth Islands Historical Society)

ed to have been slain." Epenow recognized Dermer, and the Indians attacked. The English escaped, but Dermer died of his wounds on his way to Virginia.

Gosnold had imagined that the English could settle this bountiful land, living harmoniously with the people who already made it their home. Gosnold's hope was short-lived. After his death, Gosnold's Hope became Buzzards Bay, for the ospreys that hunt in its waters. Some names had more staying power. His sailors gave Cape Cod its name. Shoal Hope and Gosnold's Hope were no more, but years later the Puritan minister Cotton Mather predicted that Cape Cod was "a name which I suppose it will never lose till shoals of codfish be seen swimming on its highest hills." ᴐ

2

they knew they were pilgrims

THE PLAGUE BROUGHT by European sailors devastated the Native people of New England, and the Cape was particularly hard hit. Leadership among the surviving fractured communities passed to younger men: Aspinet at Nauset, Iyanough at Cummaquid, and Canacum at Manomet. They did not know that another change was imminent. A group of Europeans—not merchants or sailors—was coming to their world to stay.

Pastor John Robinson led a community of English exiles in Holland. These deeply religious men and women had fled England in 1608, rejecting the pageantry and hierarchy of the Church of England to put their faith in God's almighty power. Among them were a Yorkshire postmaster, William Brewster, the former secretary to Queen Elizabeth's secretary of state, and the orphan William Bradford. Brewster's wife had been jailed for religious dissent, and he narrowly escaped prison. Safely in Holland, they found Leyden to be "A fair and beautiful city of sweet situation."

But these pious refugees were alarmed as their children grew up adopting liberal Dutch attitudes; they even signed aboard Dutch ships and joined the Dutch army. Yearning to free their children from such influences, they sought their own colony somewhere outside Europe. They contacted the proprietors of Jamestown; they considered the Dutch East India Company's offer to send them to Guiana or South Africa. Then they learned that the Plymouth Company, then the Council for New England, had a grant to everything between the fortieth and forty-eighth latitudes, roughly from New Jersey to Nova Scotia. Despite its reportedly harsh climate, they considered New England.

The Council for New England wanted settlers to exploit New World resources. By July 1620 the Council and the Leyden congregation had reached a bargain. The Council would outfit two ships, and the congregation would go to the New World. For seven years the settlers would work for the Council; after that, they could either pay off their debt or continue as the Council directed.

Reverend Robinson bid his congregation farewell as they boarded the *Speedwell* on July 20. Bradford was sorry to leave "that godly and pleasant city" of Leyden, "but they knew they were Pilgrims, and looked not much on those things, but lift up their eyes to the heavens."

Ninety more emigrants waited at Southampton on the second ship, the *Mayflower*. Both sailed on August 15, but the leaky *Speedwell* forced both back. After more than a week of repairs, it became clear that the *Speedwell* could not cross the Atlantic. Both vessels put into Plymouth, England, where many decided to stay. But 102 others crowded aboard the *Mayflower* on September 6, 1620, for the Atlantic voyage.

For the next sixty-five miserable days dead calm alternated with violent storms, one of which snapped the *Mayflower*'s main beam. Fortunately, they had packed a house jack that kept the ship stable. On November 10 they spied land—the Highlands of Truro. They

Max Bohm, *Study for Pilgrim Mural*, c. 1920: the Pilgrims have an election—the foundation of self-government. (Collection of the Town of Provincetown, courtesy Provincetown Art Commission)

turned south toward New Jersey. But "they conceived themselves in great danger" from the "deangerous shoulds and roring breakers" of Monomoy, so Captain Christopher Jones turned north. On Saturday morning, November 11, 1620 (old style; November 21 by today's calendar), "hapy to gett out of those dangers before night overtooke them, as by God's providence they did," they sailed into Provincetown Harbor.

Many of the non-Pilgrims, particularly the indentured servants, still wanted to go south, even more so now that they had a taste of New England November. Objecting to the bitter cold, they pointed to their contracts—they were to serve in Virginia or along the Hudson. Bradford and Brewster and other Pilgrim leaders diplomatically pacified them. Meeting in the *Mayflower* cabin in Provincetown harbor, all signed a compact, "solemnly and mutually" agreeing to "combine ourselves into a civil body politic, for our better ordering and Preservation." They agreed to "enact, constitute, and frame such just and equal laws" as were "most meete and convenient for the generall good" and to obey these laws. They agreed that the members of the colony would choose a governor from among themselves, and they confirmed John Carver's appointment as governor.

This agreement, the Mayflower Compact, is the beginning of self-government in the New World. Spanish, French, and Dutch colonies, and the English outpost at Jamestown, were governed from the Old World. Even in Europe, people had no voice in their own government; they were bound by laws and customs they had not made, ruled by men or women they had not chosen. But this community would make its own laws and choose its own governors.

That afternoon sixteen men went ashore for firewood. They stayed aboard the next day, the Sabbath, offering prayers and thanks for their safe deliverance. On Monday the women went ashore to do their laundry, as the men unpacked their sailing shallop. While the battered

After sixty-five days at sea, and four months traveling, the Pilgrims are able to do laundry on the Provincetown beach.

shallop was being repaired, their military leader, Myles Standish, set off on foot with fifteen men.

Eighteen years earlier, Native people had greeted Gosnold, eager to trade. Foreigners since had cheated, killed, and kidnapped the Natives. They now watched from secure places as Standish and his men walked the shore. Standish saw five or six men and a dog farther down the beach, but all fled into the woods. The Pilgrims hoped to show that they came in peace, but could find no Natives to convince.

They walked until nightfall, discovering no sign of Natives. After camping on the beach, the next morning they marched up the Pamet River. Here were fifty or sixty acres of cleared ground and a recently harvested cornfield. They took a large iron pot from a dwelling, and in the sand nearby uncovered baskets of corn buried for the winter. Piling corn into the kettle and stuffing it into their pockets, they carried it off. They also found many fresh graves of the plague's victims.

A much-needed spring, their first fresh water since leaving England, restored them. Near the ruins of what appeared to be a European fort they found canoes. As night fell on the short November day they made their camp beside a pond in what is now Truro. They sank the iron kettle into the pond to hide it from the

Indians, though why they did is a mystery. Perhaps the Indians should have hidden the kettle first.

The next morning they marched back to the *Mayflower,* where the others were repairing the shallop and cutting firewood. Captain Jones told the Pilgrims that the plentiful blackfish, or pilot whales, would provide enough oil to pay off the investors. But the Pilgrims were farmers, not fishermen, and did not trust the sea.

Ten days later Jones led thirty-three men in the shallop and long-boats back to the Pamet River. They walked back to where they had found the corn—they called it Corn Hill, and so it is still called—but the ground was frozen and covered in snow. They had not brought shovels. Using their swords, they dug out ten bushels of corn and beans.

They did not find any Indian villages, but they did find two *wetus,* or wigwams—still occupied but with no sign of residents. Digging for corn, they found a grave of a blond man and his child, possibly one of the shipwrecked Frenchmen. Some suggested building their colony on Corn Hill. It was fertile, was easy to defend, and had fresh water. But the ship's pilot, Thomas Coppin, had been there before and told them of a better place across Cape Cod Bay. English sailors called it "Thievish Harbor," but the Native people had called it Patuxet. John Smith's map labeled it Plymouth. The party returned to the *Mayflower.*

The Pilgrims helped themselves to the Indians' corn and named the place Corn Hill. Painting by Frank Milby.

Corn Hill, Truro, as Edward Hopper saw it in 1930. (Courtesy McNay Art Museum, San Antonio)

They did not leave the ship again for twelve days. It was bitterly cold when Standish and fourteen men sailed the shallop down toward Nauset. Late in the day they saw some Nausets cutting up a pilot whale onshore. The Pilgrims beached their shallop five miles away and built a small camp. They marched inland, found abandoned wigwams, cornfields unplanted that year, and more Indian graves. They marched back to the beach.

At midnight piercing shrieks surrounded them in the darkness; two Pilgrims fired their muskets and the weird sounds ceased. Before dawn, some men prepared breakfast as the others moved supplies back to the boats, beached on the tidal flats. Suddenly, shrieks cut through the morning as thirty Indians came out of the woods. Arrows flew through the air. The Pilgrims had already packed most of their weapons; those who had guns fired into the woods, others ran for the boats. Retrieving their muskets, the Pilgrims shot at the Nausets, all but one of them melting back into the woods. He continued to fire arrows, then vanished into the woods as Standish shot a tree and showered him with splinters.

Standish and the men pursued him for a quarter mile. Back at camp they found eighteen arrows, tipped with brass, antlers, or eagle claws. They would continue exploring for five days but would see no more Natives. They called this area First Encounter.

Back in the shallop, they sailed for Plymouth, which Coppin, the pilot, had previously visited. They found its fine harbor, smaller than Provincetown's, and cleared cornfields, but there was no sign of inhabitants. They returned to the *Mayflower.* While they were gone, Bradford's wife, Dorothy, had fallen off the *Mayflower* and drowned in Provincetown's frigid harbor. Her body was not recovered. Three other passengers had died as the *Mayflower* waited. Their bodies were carried ashore and buried on a hillside. They now lie somewhere under the pavement of Bradford Street.

After five weeks on Cape Cod, on December 15 they sailed for Plymouth. The Pilgrims, with their eyes fixed on the next world, had little curiosity about this one. In five weeks on the Cape they had made it as far as Eastham; they would not return to the Cape for six months.

But they were not tourists. They needed to focus on surviving. No one with a choice would have started a New England colony in December. More than half of the 102 Pilgrims died over the winter. They built a stronghouse, a few huts, and a barricade fence, knowing the Indians were watching and fearing an attack. In March an Indian strode into their tiny settlement. The surviving Pilgrims barricaded themselves in their stronghouse. He pounded on the door, shouting,

"Welcome, Englishmen!" Samoset had lived on the coast of Maine, learning English from traders and fishermen. Now he came as an emissary from the Wampanoag sachem Massassoit. He returned a few days later with four more Indians, including Tisquantum. They arranged for peace negotiations with Massassoit, who agreed that his people, including the Cape Indians, would trade furs only with

The Last Indian, a lithograph by Lucy L'Engle. (Collection of the Town of Provincetown, courtesy Provincetown Art Commission)

these Pilgrims. Tisquantum and Samoset showed the Pilgrims how to plant corn.

The Pilgrims were not great explorers. Twelve-year-old John Billington, from what Bradford called "one of ye profanest families amongst them," wandered away from both his dysfunctional family and the Pilgrims. He spent days lost in the woods; he was found by an Indian and taken to Canacum, at Manomet. Canacum sent the boy to the Nausets, knowing they had lost men to the English seven years earlier.

After searching futilely for young Billington, the Pilgrims went to Massassoit. He knew where the boy was. Six Pilgrims, Tisquantum, and Tokamahamon sailed for Nauset. A sudden thunderstorm forced them to spend the night inside the sandy neck of Cummaquid. When they awoke their shallop was aground on the flats. Across the channel they saw Indians, the Mattacheesets, or people of the old marshes, gathering lobsters. Tisquantum and Tokamahamon went to talk, and all were invited to breakfast with their sachem, Iyanough.

Iyanough was "a man not exceeding twenty-six year of age," according to the Pilgrim Edward Winslow, "but very personable, gentle, courteous, and fair conditioned, indeed not like a savage, save for his attire." Iyanough's "entertainment was answerable to his parts, and his cheer plentiful and various."

But their breakfast had a "grievous" interruption. An old woman, "whom we judged to be no less than an hundred years old," came to see the English. When she saw them she broke "forth into great passion, weeping and crying excessively." What upset her? "They told us, she had three sons, who, when Master Hunt was in these parts, went aboard his ship to trade with him, and he carried them captives to Spain." None had returned. She was "deprived of the comfort of her children in her old age."

Winslow told the woman—and all present—that they "were sorry that any Englishman should give them that offense, that Hunt was a bad man, and that all the English that heard of it condemned him." Even "though it would gain us all the skins in the country," they would never do so evil a deed.

After breakfast Iyanough and two of his men joined the sail to Nauset. The tide was out that evening when they approached First

Iyanough

OCCUPATION: Sachem of the
Cummaquid

LIFETIME: c. 1595–1623

HOMETOWNS: Cummaquid and
Mattacheese, now Barnstable.

FAMILY: Son of Iyanough,
sachem of Cummaquid. Married
Mary No-Pee, daughter of
Canacum, sachem of the
Narragansetts; daughter Mary
Little Dove, son John Hyanno.

Iyanough, the leader who aided the
Pilgrims and suffered for it. Sketch by
David Lewis for a statue of Iyanough.
(Courtesy Cape Cod Community
College)

Encounter beach, so Iyanough, Tisquantum, and two Indians waded
ashore to meet the Nauset sachem, Aspinet. After sunset they
returned with Aspinet and more than a hundred warriors. Some of
these men, Nausets and Pilgrims, may have encountered one another
in December on this same beach.

Aspinet left his weapons and half his men onshore as he accompanied Tisquantum and Iyanough to the shallop. A Nauset warrior carried young John Billington, "behung with beads," and placed him in
the boat. Winslow gave knives to Aspinet and the Nausets who had
taken in Billington.

Meanwhile, the Narragansetts kidnapped Massassoit. After his
release, Massassoit accused Tisquantum of conspiring against him.

Following Wampanoag protocol, he sent a party to execute Tisquantum in Plymouth. Bradford, now the governor, protected his ally by taking him on a trading mission to Monomoy. There a sudden fever killed Tisquantum.

Bradford could not afford to alienate Massassoit, though his protection of Tisquantum threatened to do this. The Pilgrims depended on Indian trade, both for food to survive and for furs to pay off their English investors. The Pilgrims expanded a Native trade route up Scusset Creek and across an easy portage to the Manomet River to Buzzards Bay. Near the portage, at Aptucxet ("at the little strait and tidal river"), they built a trading post that thrived for thirty years.

Manomet was a crucial link in this trade, and the sachem Canacum an important ally. Bradford happened to be at Manomet in January

The Pilgrims built a trading post at Aptucxet, 1627; this re-creation was built three centuries later. (Courtesy Boston Athenaeum)

1623, along with his new translator, Hobbamock, when a Monomoy delegation came to call on Canacum. Hosts and visitors, as was customary, silently smoked a pipe. After all had smoked, the Monomoys presented Canacum with a basket of tobacco and wampum. Then they explained why they had come. Their shaman, or "powwow," had been gambling with a stranger. During the game "they became greatly enraged" and the powwow had killed the stranger. Now the stranger's people were demanding the powwow's death. If the Monomoys did not kill him, they would attack the Monomoys. What did Canacum advise?

After a period of silence Canacum asked opinions. Everyone, even Hobbamock and Bradford, was allowed to speak. Bradford withheld his opinion, but all who spoke agreed that the powwow must die. Innocent people would suffer if he was allowed to live, and "he had deserved it and the rest were innocent"; it was "better that one should die than many." The Monomoys left with this advice.

Later that same year Myles Standish was buying corn from Canacum when a visitor, an emissary from Wittawumet of Wessaguscus, came with a plan to destroy the English outpost at Wessaguscus (now Weymouth). The English there were not Pilgrims but "adventurers," traders sent by the Council for New England. Wittawumet hoped to enlist Canacum's support.

Myles Standish went back to Plymouth convinced that the Manomets, Iyanough's Cummaquids (Iyanough was Canacum's son-in-law), the Nausets, and the Pamets were all preparing to attack. Standish, who is our only source that a conspiracy existed, suspected that Massassoit himself was involved, and that the Indians would attack Plymouth first, to prevent retaliation after the destruction of Wessaguscus.

Rather than wait for an attack, Standish struck first. He called the sachem Wittawumet to a parley. When Wittawumet arrived, Standish killed him and his two aides, cut off Wittawumet's head, and hung it as a warning on Plymouth's gate.

Aspinet, Iyanough, and Canacum took to the swamps to avoid Standish's wrath. There they contracted fevers and died. Iyanough, the Pilgrim's former friend, "in the midst of these distractions, said the God of the English was offended with them, and would destroy them in his anger." Other Cape Indians stayed hidden, neglecting their farms, and sickness returned. Winslow thought it "strange to hear" how many "still daily die among them." He thought the Indians would all perish "because through fear" of Standish "they set little or no corn, which is the staff of life, and without which they cannot long preserve health and strength."

Standish's preemptive strike destroyed much of the Indian strength on the Cape. It also brought a reproach from the Reverend John Robinson, in Holland. "Concerning the killing of those poor Indians. . . . Oh! How happy a thing had it been if you had converted some, before you had killed any." Robinson remarked to his flock that "where blood is once begun to be shed, it is seldom staunched off a long time after."

He reminded Bradford that the Pilgrims were not "magistrates" over the Indians, and he cautioned him to "seriously consider the disposition" of Myles Standish, who he feared lacked "the tenderness of life of man." Being "a terror to poor barbarous people" was "more glorious in men's eyes, than pleasing in God's."

Robinson hoped to come to Plymouth to make his flock more pleasing in God's eyes. But he died in 1625. By this time, with Iyanough, Aspinet, and Canacum dead, the lives of the people of the Cape were changed forever. ◦

3

then that land is ours

THE WAMPANOAGS and Narragansetts to the west kept Plymouth from expanding in that direction; when Puritans arrived in Boston in 1630 the north was also closed beyond Duxbury and Scituate. The destruction of the Cape's Native peoples opened the possibility of eastward expansion.

Plymouth granted Cape lands in the 1630s to interested settlers, but only if they continued to live in the colony. A Mayflower passenger, Stephen Hopkins, was allowed to cut hay at Mattacheese, Iyanough's "old fields," provided he still lived in Plymouth.

The Cape's oldest house, dating from the 1600s, in Sandwich. The Hoxie House gets its name from a nineteenth-century whaling captain who lived in it two centuries after it was built.

In April 1637 Plymouth gave ten men of Saugus, north of Boston, "liberty to view a place to sit down on" at Shawme, the "trail going east." Led by Edmund and Elizabeth Freeman and their two sons, the families called their settlement Sandwich. It became the fourth town in Plymouth Colony.

Later that year the Reverend Stephen Bachiler led another group to the marshes of Mattacheese. Bachiler, "a man of learning and ingenuity," was in his seventies; he had been ejected as pastor of an English parish for nonconformity. He had gone to Holland before crossing the Atlantic, arriving in Lynn with his children, grandchildren, and other followers. Pilgrims and Puritans empathized until they discovered the full range of Bachiler's nonconformity. Shocked by "his contempt for authority," Massachusetts leaders ordered Bachiler "to forbeare exercising his gifts as a pastor or teacher" except to his immediate family "until some scandles be removed." But more "scandles" arose.

Bachiler and his sect arrived on foot in Mattacheese in 1637 but stayed only the winter. Moving to New Hampshire in the spring of 1638, the elderly Bachiler, despite his own (in John Winthrop's words) "lusty comely" wife, "did solicit the chastity of his neighbor's wife." He was excommunicated. He later remarried, at the age of eighty-nine, after his lusty and comely wife died. This new wife was later given thirty-nine lashes and "branded with the letter A" for adultery with a neighbor. Bachiler abandoned his branded, unfaithful bride, returned to England, and married again. She filed for divorce.

Plymouth wanted a stable community, not a refuge for lusty ministers. The minister John Lothrop's "Competent measure of Gifts" and "Great Measure of brokenes of hart and humilities of sperritt" set him apart from Bachiler. He settled at Mattacheese in 1639, changing its name to Barnstable.

As Lothrop's band settled at Barnstable, Anthony Thacher and his wife led another group to Yarmouth. The Thachers had lost four children and a boat when a storm smashed their vessel on a rocky outcropping off Marblehead—now Thacher's Island. Little wonder that the Thachers came to the Cape on foot.

The sea was dangerous, and these new Cape Codders avoided it. Land and farming were the focus of their worldly ambition. Fish were abundant, but the settlers of Sandwich, Barnstable, and Yarmouth raised corn, sheep, cattle, and pigs, harvesting salt hay to feed the cattle. Plymouth had one boat, which it sent to catch fish in Provincetown—using the fish to fertilize corn, not to eat or trade. They would take oil when a whale drifted ashore, but they would not pursue whales off the coast.

Plymouth residents worried that fast-growing Massachusetts Bay would overwhelm the Cape, and so they reserved the area east of Yarmouth for purchase by Old Comers, those who had come over on the *Mayflower* (1620), *Fortune* (1621), or *Anne* (1623). This completed the complicated arrangement Bradford and the Plymouth leaders made when they bought out the London investors in 1627. Under the original agreement, the initial settlers would get half the colony when Plymouth paid off its debt. Rather than divide the colony, Bradford

The Pilgrims would not hunt whales, but would harvest oil when a whale beached itself.

gave these Old Comers the right to purchase land in this tract stretching from Yarmouth to Monomoy. The Indians, unaware of deals between Pilgrim settlers and London investors, still had possession.

Fearing a dispersal of the Plymouth community, Bradford sent Thomas Prence in 1641 to scout Nauset as a better place for the entire colony. From Plymouth the Pilgrims were migrating to Sandwich and Duxbury; perhaps if Nauset could support everyone, they would not have to move away. Prence reported that Nauset could not support the entire colony; but he did buy land for himself, and in 1644 he led seven families to found Eastham.

Prence had arrived in Plymouth in 1621 and married Elder Brewster's daughter Patience; when she died of smallpox, he married Mary Collier, daughter of Plymouth's richest man. He had been governor and would be again. Though the law required governors to live in Plymouth, Prence governed from Eastham from 1657 until his death in 1673.

After buying Nauset, Prence asked the sachems, "Who owns Billingsgate?" No one owned it, the Nausets replied. "Then that land is ours," Prence said. The Nausets agreed. Nausets and Pilgrims had different concepts of ownership. For the Nausets, no one owned land; it belonged to everyone. So yes, it was the Pilgrims', as much as it was everyone else's. But for the Pilgrims, ownership was exclusive. The Pilgrims were more effective than the Nausets in enforcing their notion of ownership.

Governor Thomas Prence built this house in 1646; by the early twentieth century it was used to house pigs. (Courtesy Chatham Historical Society)

The Pilgrims' cattle overran the Indians' cornfields, and the Pilgrims cut the trees. Here cattle water in Bennett's Pond, Provincetown. (Courtesy Historic New England)

Years later, an Indian named Lieutenant Anthony came to Plymouth to claim Billingsgate. The Nausets had not owned it after all; his people had. The Pilgrims bought him off. (Lieutenant Island in Wellfleet is named for him.) Reflecting on this transaction, Henry David Thoreau speculated, "Who knows but a Lieutenant Anthony may be knocking at the door of the White House some day?"

Using the land was as much a point of disagreement as owning it. The Indians raised corn, the English raised cattle, sheep, and pigs. Turned loose to forage, the English animals ate the corn, as well as the shrubs and grass that held the thin layer of topsoil in place. The topsoil blew out to sea, leaving Indians and English both struggling for survival in the newly barren land.

The Indians had taught the English to harvest cranberries, grow corn, and catch whales. Some of the more adventurous settlers set out with the Indians in canoes to bring back whales for their valuable oil. But farming was the real work of the English on Cape Cod. The English in the rest of Massachusetts took more enthusiastically to fishing, particularly for cod. They built boats with the ample lumber of the mainland and caught cod and sold it in the West Indies. Massachusetts boomed as a trading center, whereas Cape Codders continued trying to coax corn from the sandy soil.

Even when Governor Prence bought the Cape's tip from the sachem Samson, the Plymouth settlers did not pursue fishing with any zeal. Prence gave Samson two brass kettles, six coats, a dozen axes, hoes, knives, and a box for the harbor and the surrounding land, both to be held in common by the entire colony. The Pilgrims took turns fishing in their one shallop, selling fishing rights for one shilling on every barrel of fish caught. This shilling supported the one school in the colony, at Plymouth.

Despite the fact that land could not be owned individually, a settlement emerged here, much different from the communities created at Barnstable, Sandwich, Eastham, and Yarmouth. The nearest government, spiritual or temporal, was far away. Thomas Hinckley of Barnstable complained that the Cape's tip was a nest of smugglers and fishermen, as well as "covetous English" who sold liquor to the Indians.

Provincetown's fishermen and smugglers were not the only newcomers upsetting the Pilgrims. William Nickerson came to Yarmouth around 1641 and bought Monomoy from the sachem Mattaquason, paying him with a shallop, half a dozen kettles, axes, hoes, knives, forty shillings' worth of wampum, twelve shillings in cash, ten coats, and a hat. Plymouth summoned him to court in 1656 for buying Indian land without permission and for selling Mattaquason a boat. Fined five pounds for every acre he had bought (estimates ranged up to four thousand acres), he was also ordered to pay Plymouth for the land, which it claimed to hold in trust for the Old Comers.

Richard Sears, a *Mayflower* passenger and one of the founders of Yarmouth, was constantly in litigation against William Nickerson. (Courtesy Chatham Historical Society)

This set off a generation of litigation. For the next eighteen years Nickerson sued Plymouth's leaders, the sachem Mattaquason, and even his own son-in-law before the issues were settled. Since Nickerson's suits against Plymouth were heard in Plymouth courts, he generally lost. He was stripped of all but one hundred acres, for which he had to pay Plymouth ninety pounds. The court awarded the rest to a consortium led by Barnstable's Thomas Hinckley, Prence's successor as governor. Nickerson fought on, attacking Plymouth in letters to New York's governor (who claimed Nantucket and Martha's Vineyard). In the end he bought four thousand acres, which in 1712 became the town of Chatham.

While Prence and Nickerson bought up this world, others sought a path to the next. The "Family of Love," or Familists, brought what the Pilgrims regarded as "Strange & heretical tenets" to Barnstable in 1641. Barnstable sent them to Rhode Island and thanked God with fasting and humiliation for their deliverance. Even the more tolerant Rhode Island whipped one of the Familists, Samuel Groton, for calling magistrates "just-asses." Anabaptists arrived three years later, expelled from Boston for opposing infant baptism. Barnstable rejected Familists but allowed Anabaptists.

Barnstable's Congregational church excommunicated Goodwife Shelley in 1649 for calling Sisters Wells and Dimmock "proud" and for refusing to attend her trial for the offense. Wells and Dimmock, she said, started the trouble by having a "christian meeting" and not inviting her. A few years later Shelley's daughter Hannah confessed to "toutching carnall & uncleane carriages" with David Linnell; though they had since married, both were excommunicated and publicly flogged.

These were signs of trouble in the Cape's churches. Barnstable had a long schism after Reverend Lothrop's death in 1653, the Sandwich pulpit was vacant for four years, and Yarmouth's congregation constantly squabbled. Into this religious confusion came two English Quakers, Christopher Holder and John Copeland, fresh from a Boston jail and a Rhode Island exile. Hearing of Sandwich's troubles, they approached by way of Martha's Vineyard, which banished them. An Indian took them by canoe to Woods Hole. Holder preached so effectively in a wooded Sandwich valley still called Christopher's Hollow that eighteen families became Quakers.

Quakerism took such a hold in Sandwich that Barnstable's John Cudworth, a former member of Lothrop's church, wrote, "The

Sandwich men may not go to the Bay [Boston], lest they be taken up for Quakers." Cudworth, a governor's assistant, seemed too sympa thetic to suspected Quakers; he was replaced by the hard-liner Thomas Hinckley. "Hinckley's Law" fined Quakers and mandated church attendance.

Sensing that the Cape would be fertile Quaker territory, Governor Prence forbade Sandwich to harbor them. Any Quaker coming into any town would be given fifteen lashes and ordered out. Anyone hosting, attending, or preaching at a Quaker meeting would be fined forty shillings; the fine for entertaining a Quaker was five pounds. From 1658 to 1671 Plymouth collected seven hundred pounds (over 2 million dollars today) in fines and property from Quakers and those who entertained them.

Constable George Barlow arrested Copeland and Holder three days after they arrived in Sandwich. Irate that the magistrates would not let him whip the Quakers, Barlow took them to Barnstable to be properly flogged. Each received thirty-three lashes with "a new tormenting whip with three cords and knots at each end."

Fearful that whipping the Quaker leaders was not enough, officials sent Isaac Robinson, son of the late Reverend John Robinson, to Sandwich to "seduce them from the error of their ways." It did not work. Robinson returned to Barnstable urging that the Sandwich Quakers be permitted to worship freely. Denounced as a "manifest opposer of the laws," he was disenfranchised and dropped from the roster of freemen. He fled to Suckanesset, now Falmouth, beyond Plymouth's reach.

"What a God have the English," an Indian commented, "who deal so with one another about their God!" Robinson's father had left England to escape religious oppression; he left Barnstable to escape the oppression of his father's congregation. Commissioner Edward Randolph, sent from England to investigate New England, told Governor Hinckley that it made as much sense for Plymouth to tax Quakers to support Congregational churches as it would to tax Plymouth Congregationalists to pay the Church of England minister "who now preaches in Boston and you hear him not."

Hearing Randolph's report on the persecution of Quakers and other outrages, King James II consolidated all of New England into one dominion. The dominion did not last, but the union of

Massachusetts and Plymouth did. When Massachusetts received a new charter in 1691, Plymouth was included in its territory.

By this time the native people on the Cape were also subject to English law and economy. As the English fenced off and constricted the land, the Indians began to object. Still, Governor Josiah Winslow in 1676 wrote, "I think I can clearly say that the English did not possess one foot of land in this colony but what was fairly obtained by honest purchase of the Indian proprietors."

Paupmumuck, the sachem of the South Sea Indians ("South Sea" was the original name for Nantucket Sound) in Massippee, sold his land in 1648 to Barnstable settlers. Myles Standish negotiated the deal, giving Paupmumuck two brass kettles, a bushel of corn, and half the fence he would need to enclose his remaining thirty acres. He was to have "free leave and Liberty" to hunt and trap on the lands he sold.

Ten years later Paupmumuck realized he had given away too much, as there now was a barrier between different South Sea Indian groups. He complained to three English leaders, Winslow, John Alden, and Richard Bourne. Winslow and Alden patiently explained that a deal was a deal. Bourne, a lawyer and Sandwich selectman, disagreed. He thought that Standish had taken advantage of Paupmumuck.

Bourne envisioned creating a refuge where the Indians could protect themselves from the avaricious duplicity of the whites. Granting land around Mashpee Pond, and another sixty square miles in Mashpee, Bourne made the area a haven for the Native people living in it, and others who would become Christians and settle there. Sachems Wepquish and Tookenchosin, from Mashpee and Cotuit, and Quatchatisset of Manomet all ceded their lands to what was called the Mashpee kingdom.

Bourne believed that the traditional Indian social and political structure—dispersed settlements, no clear lines of authority—weakened it against white pressure. Whites took advantage of the divisions to buy land from "leaders" with no authority to sell, or simply took land (as they had at Billingsgate) if no one "owned" it. Bourne envisioned Mashpee as a self-governing Indian community, advised by Bourne, but under the leadership of the six sachems. John Cotton, a leading Puritan divine, and John Eliot, the "apostle to the Indians" who translated the

Bible into the Algonquian language and organized Christian Indians into "Praying Towns," ordained Bourne as a minister in 1670.

By Bourne's count, in 1674 there were only ninety-five "Praying Indians" at Mashpee. But the next year, when war broke out between the English and the Wampanoags, led by Massassoit's son Metacom, or Philip, the Cape Indians sided with the English. Elsewhere in New England the Indians rose up and destroyed white settlements, in one of the most devastating conflicts in American history, King Philip's War. When it ended in 1676, nine thousand New Englanders, English and Indian, were dead. Mashpee became a haven for Indians, who built a meetinghouse, now the oldest house of worship on Cape Cod and one of the oldest in the United States.

Bourne became a cultural hero to the Mashpees. One legend has Bourne wrestling with the devil, who is taunted by a chickadee, in a verse that became a favorite jump-rope rhyme into the nineteenth century. The chickadee sings:

Howdy, Giant,
Howdy, Devil.
You're gonna wressle
With Richard Bourne.
You're gonna git
The worst of it.
You're gonna git
The worst of it.

The devil gathered stones to pelt the bird, but he tripped and dropped the rocks, which explains why there are rocks at Bournedale but not on the outer Cape. When Bourne died, an Indian, Simon Popmonit, succeeded him as minister.

Mashpee constantly had to defend its territory from encroachments by other Cape towns. The Provincial Assembly in 1746 appointed three white guardians for the Mashpees, authorizing them to sell Mashpee lands. When the Mashpees protested, the Assembly ignored them. The Mashpees sent one of their own, Reuben Cognehew, to present their grievances to the king. Cognehew sailed from Rhode Island; the captain sailed for the West Indies hoping to sell him into slavery. Cognehew escaped that trap but was impressed onto a British warship in Jamaica. A British admiral heard his case, and Cognehew

The Indian Meeting House in Mashpee, built in 1684.

The windmill in South Yarmouth, early in the twentieth century.

The Cape's oldest windmill has been in Eastham since 1793, but it was built in Plymouth in 1680 and moved to Truro in 1770.

Brewster gristmill.

finally reached England in 1760. After an investigation, King George III sided with the Mashpees and forced the Massachusetts Assembly to allow the Mashpees to continue to govern themselves.

This was one of the great events for Cape Cod in the eighteenth century. Otherwise, the settlements grew, and the towns had their political squabbles, mainly ecclesiastical—how to pay the minister, whether the minister was worth paying. But neither the towns nor the everyday lives of people changed much between King Philip's War and the American Revolution. People bought and sold land, harvested cranberries and coaxed corn out of the sandy soil, ground the corn at the windmills, and stripped blubber from stranded whales. ◠

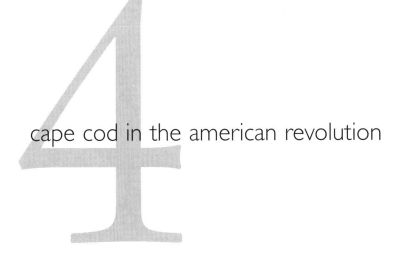

cape cod in the american revolution

BY 1770 THE CAPE'S ten towns were home to about 14,000 people, fewer than lived in Boston. The more ambitious rose to the top of the small farming communities or moved out. The Otis family of Barnstable was an example of a family that succeeded.

Colonel James Otis moderated Barnstable's Town Meeting, commanded the militia, sat as a judge, and when the town elected him to the Assembly, the Assembly made him their speaker. By the 1770s his children were established in their own careers. His son

Joseph stayed in Barnstable, succeeded the colonel as commander of the militia, and was one of the Cape's leading radicals. His daughter Mercy married James Warren of Plymouth, soon to be speaker of the Provincial Assembly. A confidante of John and Abigail Adams, Mercy Otis Warren wrote a series of scathing attacks on the royal government. The colonel's son James Otis Jr., a Boston lawyer known as "the Patriot," coined the phrase "Taxation without Representation is Tyranny."

But when Boston in 1773 called on other towns to form Committees of Correspondence, to keep in touch with Boston's radicals on the growing crisis with England—James Otis Jr. was on the Boston Committee—Barnstable flatly refused. Everyone knew that the Otises supported this step. But another influential Barnstable man, Edward Bacon, opposed it.

Bacon told the Barnstable Town Meeting that the members of Boston's committee "were the vilest of men, that it was Scandalous to Correspond with them." He apologized when he learned that the younger Otis was on the committee (though not active—a mental breakdown limited Otis's activities, but the committee still used his

James and Mary Aleyne Otis, of Barnstable, were painted by John Singleton Copley in 1760. He was Speaker of the Massachusetts House of Representatives, a judge, and moderator of Barnstable's Town Meeting. Her grandfather arrived on the *Mayflower;* their thirteen children included the lawyer and Patriot James Otis, the writer Mercy Otis Warren, Samuel Aleyne Otis, the first clerk of the U.S. Senate, and Joseph Otis, a Barnstable militia captain; a grandson would be mayor of Boston. (Courtesy Roland P. Murdock Collection, Wichita Art Museum)

The West Parish of Barnstable stands on land given by John Crocker; the Revere bell was donated by the Otis family. Opened in 1719 and the tower added in the 1720s, the meetinghouse was restored in the twentieth century, thanks to Elizabeth Crocker Jenkins.

name). Bacon stood by his description of the other members, naming three, William Molineux, William Dennie, and the Reverend Samuel Cooper, as "men of very bad characters," as "one was an Atheist, one Never Went to Meeting, and the other was incontinent."

Molineux learned what Bacon had said and reported to the committee's leader, Samuel Adams. Adams was not surprised that "enemies of the public liberty" opposed the Committees of Correspondence. "Whether Mr. B. is of this character is a question in which his Constituents ought certainly to satisfy themselves beyond a reasonable doubt," Adams wrote to Colonel Otis. "A man's professions may be as he pleases; but I honestly confess I cannot easily believe him to be a sincere friend to his Country, who can upon any consideration be prevail'd on to associate with so detestable an enemy" as opponents of Committees of Correspondence.

Barnstable voters stood by Bacon. They would not form a Committee of Correspondence, and they elected Bacon to the Assembly. There he voted to create a provincial Committee of Correspondence to communicate with other colonies. He favored communication, but he opposed incontinent atheists.

Boston's Sons of Liberty (Molineux was a leader) brought on a new crisis in December 1773 by destroying three shiploads of tea in Boston Harbor. A fourth ship, the *William*, had run aground off Provincetown. Jonathan Clarke of Boston, a tea agent, sailed to Provincetown, and with the assistance of a Wellfleet man rounded up most of the tea. "As the

People in Boston have thou't themselves at Liberty to destroy what Tea was there," he wrote to his father, "I fear the people within this place think themselves licensed to steal what is here." He recovered all but a few crates.

Boston's destruction of the tea provoked Parliament to suspend Massachusetts' government, close Boston's harbor, forbid Town Meetings unless the governor approved them, and give the governor, not the towns, the power to appoint sheriffs and magistrates. The Committees of Correspondence labeled these the "Intolerable Acts," meant to subdue the people of Massachusetts.

The radicals determined to protest these acts by preventing courts from sitting. In September 1774 the Court of Common Pleas would convene at Barnstable, with Judge James Otis presiding over eighteen judges. Fifteen hundred men from Barnstable, Bristol, and Plymouth counties gathered in Sandwich the night before. Raising a liberty pole, they pledged to "observe an orderly, circumspect, and civil behavior" toward strangers and each other. The next morning, calling themselves "the body of the people," they marched to Barnstable. They raised their hats in salute as they passed Otis's house.

"Gentleman," Otis asked when he reached the courthouse, finding it surrounded, "what is the purpose for which this vast assemblage is collected here?"

Dr. Nathaniel Freeman of Sandwich, "in a loud clear voice," replied: "May it please your honor, oppressed by a view of the dangers with which we are surrounded, and terrified by the horribly black cloud which is suspended over our heads and ready to burst upon us,—our safety, all that is dear to us, and the welfare of unborn millions, have directed this movement to prevent the court from being opened or doing any business. We have taken the consequences into consideration; we have weighed them well, and have formed this resolution which we shall not rescind."

"This is a legal and constitutional court," Otis replied. Recent British acts had not changed it. Jurors were chosen according to Massachusetts law. "Why would you interrupt its proceedings? Why do you make a leap before you get to the hedge?"

Freeman said they trusted Otis and his court; but their decisions would be appealed to the Superior Court, where sheriffs chose jurors

The Crocker Tavern still welcomes guests. (Courtesy Anne and Bryan Carlson).

and judges sat "at the King's pleasure," paid by revenue "extorted from us by the illegal and unconstitutional edict of foreign despotism." If the despotic Superior Court judges "have no business, they can do us no harm."

Otis told them to disperse "in his Majesty's name."

"We thank your honor for having done your duty," Freeman replied; "we shall continue to perform ours."

Otis and the judges adjourned to Crocker's Inn. Back at the court-house, Freeman and Stephen Nye of Sandwich and Daniel Crocker of Barnstable drafted a statement asking the judges to "desist from all business" until a continental congress, or a provincial congress, had expressed itself.

Otis responded that the judges were "as much concerned at the late unconstitutional Acts of the British Parliament, as the People are," but thought that blocking the court "will not help the matter." If the court did not meet, how could it respond to either a provincial or continental congress? Nonetheless, thirteen judges pledged not to serve under unconstitutional Parliamentary acts.

The people were not appeased. They declared seven of the signing judges suspect. Benjamin Bourne had sold East India tea; two voted in the Assembly against calling a continental congress; Chillingsworth Foster, Harwich's assemblyman in 1768, voted against protesting the Townshend duties; Shearjashub Bourne and David Gorham showed "vanity, insolence, and audacity" by signing a "false and designing . . . flattering and fulsome" statement in support of former Governor Thomas Hutchinson, "a known Traitor, and inveterate Enemy, to the country." In this they defied all America's "united express'd sentiments" and "forfeited the esteem of the public, and enlisted under the banners of said Hutchinson, as enemies to the cause of liberty."

The judges canceled the court session. Now the crowd demanded that the judges, the sheriff, and all militia officers resign and refuse to enforce "any unconstitutional Regulations," or any "oppressive Acts of the British Parliament." They drafted confessions begging forgiveness for three judges to sign: David Gorham and Shearjashub Bourne for bidding Hutchinson farewell, and Benjamin Bourne for his "iniquitous Conduct" in selling tea. All signed their confessions, and Sheriff Nathaniel Stone pledged not to enforce laws that would "introduce an unjust and partial administration of justice" or alter Massachusetts' "free Constitution to a State of Slavery and Oppression, and to establish or encourage Popery in some Parts of British America," a reference to Parliament's Quebec Act, which allowed Catholics to practice their religion.

Though the body of the people enforced its will in Barnstable, it was soon discovered that vandals in Sandwich had cut down their liberty pole. The culprits, Benjamin Fish, Benjamin Toby, and John Jennings, were brought to Barnstable. They confessed their "hearty Sorrow and Shame," vowed never again "to oppose the Cause of Liberty," and asked forgiveness for having "justly offended all the Friends of Liberty, Justice and Virtue" by their "Enmity to the Rights and Liberties of the People," who fined them five pounds.

Barnstable held a Town Meeting in October, without the governor's permission. James Otis Sr. presided. This meeting appointed a Committee of Correspondence, reversing previous refusals. In November Otis presided at a Barnstable County congress, bringing together opponents of British policies from around the Cape. His son Joseph was the meeting's clerk.

Bacon moderated the authorized Town Meeting in January 1775. The town resolved not to pay taxes to the Boston government, but it also refused to buy weapons or send delegates to the Provincial Congress, which had replaced the suspended Assembly. Bacon said that instead of buying weapons and sending delegates, "we had better petition to the King while he was of[f]; for the time was coming when he would set up his Standard, & we should fly to it with trembling hands; & akeing hearts."

Three weeks later the senior Otis convened another Barnstable Town Meeting. This one sent a delegate to the Provincial Congress (which would choose James Warren of Plymouth, Otis's son-in-law, as its speaker). The radical *Boston Gazette* said that this second meeting showed that "the few insignificant Tories of Barnstable will hardly be able to save their BACON."

Bacon was trying to save not himself but his country. When he learned on April 20 of the "dreadful maneuvers that have taken place" at Lexington and Concord, he wrote to a friend in Plymouth of the "heart felt distress under which I now groan for the distrest scituation of my dear country."

Barnstable did not muster its militia after Lexington and Concord, but nineteen men marched off to join the militias around Boston. Six days after the battle, Otis presided over a meeting that voted to buy arms and set up military watches. When news of the Battle of Bunker Hill reached Barnstable, the Patriots raised a liberty pole and began drilling men in arms. In Falmouth, Joseph Dimmick was plowing when he heard the news of the battle. Turning the oxen over to his son, named for a British general from the Seven Years' War, Dimmick said, "Braddock, you must look to the team; I must go." His sister, steadfastly loyal to the Crown, implored him to stay.

Families and towns divided. The British army controlled Boston, the British navy the surrounding waters; the militia forces, now under George Washington's command, controlled the surrounding countryside. Patriots fled British-controlled Boston, and outlying towns drove out Loyalists. Truro Loyalists barred Reverend Upham from their homes after he entertained some visiting Patriots. When a Boston Patriot, James Perkins, died, his widow and her eight children left for her hometown of Barnstable, where these nine Patriot exiles took refuge in the home of Barnstable's leading Tory, Edward Bacon.

The Cape provided supplies for both sides. An innkeeper at Tarpaulin Cove, Elisha Nye, alerted the provincial authorities to a British sloop's raid of the Elizabeth Islands in 1775. He knew they would take a keen interest, since the Patriot official James Bowdoin owned Naushon Island. The Provincial Congress directed Captain John Grannis of Falmouth to raise thirty men (later increased to fifty) to protect the islands from British raiders.

Off Yarmouth one summer day in 1775, a British sloop lost its way. It was carrying three hundred barrels of flour to the British troops at Boston, and the captain asked some fishermen for a pilot. The Yarmouth men steered the sloop into the Bass River, unloaded it, and sent it away empty. Colonel Enoch Hallett, of the Yarmouth militia, carted the flour to Sandwich, rowed it to Scituate, and delivered it to Washington's army at Roxbury. Washington "expressed the strongest gladness at this providential occurrence," as he was down to four days' supply of bread. He praised Cape Codders, telling Hallett that the "officers and men . . . from his quarter were amongst the best men of the army."

Knowing that Washington had no boats, Cape Cod men carried whaleboats overland to Roxbury, establishing the Revolutionary navy. With these whaleboats the Patriots raided British ships in Boston Harbor and prevented the capture of livestock on Boston's Harbor Islands. Washington sent the engineer Thomas Machin to study the feasibility of a canal from Buzzards Bay to Cape Cod Bay. Machin proposed building a canal with locks at either end, estimating the cost at £32,148, 1s., 8d., or between 4 million and 9 million dollars today. The Continental Congress had other priorities in 1775 and 1776, though Washington would long continue to press for a canal.

Washington forced the British out of Boston in the spring of 1776, but Barnstable remained divided. Someone cut down Barnstable's liberty pole on the courthouse green. No culprit could be found, but many remembered hearing the sharp-tongued widow Nabby Freeman declare that "somebody ought to heave up that dead tree" every time she passed it. Since her store was next to the courthouse, she had frequently said it. They also remembered that when a committee called on her in 1773 to enlist her in the tea boycott, she had driven them from the store with her sharp tongue. They would also have known that her son Thomas was away serving in the Continental Army—he would remain in military service for the duration of the war.

After propping up their pole late at night, Barnstable's liberty lovers broke into the widow Freeman's house, dragged her from her bed, and took her to the town green. There they smeared her with tar and covered her with feathers, then set her astride a rail. Two strong young men paraded her through town. Before finally releasing the widow, they made her promise not to meddle in politics.

Tarring and feathering widows whose sons were serving in Washington's army did not help the liberty movement, which already showed signs of strain. A riot had nearly broken out on the militia training ground between Otis's supporters and the friends of Samuel and Cornelius Crocker. Though the Crockers and the Otises were both liberty men, they had long-standing personal rivalries. Otis accused the Crockers of disrespecting him. Samuel Crocker called Otis a liar. Otis and Crocker, both officers in the militia, attacked each other with their canes. Their supporters had to pull them apart.

Nathaniel Freeman, a friend of Otis's, stormed into Cornelius Crocker's home and attacked him with a cutlass. Bacon and other friends of the royal government could point to the attack on the Widow Freeman and this fight between Otis and Crocker as indications of how these liberty men would govern if the colonies won independence. Recognizing this, James Otis Sr. in May 1776 tried to apologize for the tarring and feathering of Nabby Freeman and the militia riot. The town voted not to hear his apology.

Otis's son-in-law James Warren, Speaker of the Provincial Congress, sent a broadside to all the towns in Massachusetts asking whether to declare independence. Within days Harwich, Truro, Yarmouth, and Wellfleet met and endorsed independence—the vote was unanimous in Yarmouth. But in Barnstable the Otis–Crocker feud and the attack on Nabby Freeman left the Patriots divided.

Only 65 of the 140 men attending the June 25 meeting voted on the question: Should Barnstable's representative vote for or against independence? Thirty voted for, thirty-five voted against. Embarrassed that their town alone in Massachusetts rejected independence, Joseph Otis and others printed a protest, saying it was "a matter of great grief to us that the CAUSE OF LIBERTY is treated with such indignity by some of the inhabitants of the town of Barnstable."

Captain Sturgis Gorham, who was building a privateer in his yard, responded that Barnstable had not rejected independence, but had left the decision up to its representative. Gorham did not like the aspersions that Otis cast upon the town. Otis replied in a letter to the *Boston Gazette*, charging that Gorham's and Bacon's "boisterous, illeberal behavior" had "intimidated the major part" of the people into silence. Otis said he was happy that his own "conscious integrity" and "love of my country" had "opened upon me the throats of deep mouthed mastiffs, as well as occasioned the barking of lesser curs."

In response to the charge that he and Bacon were "boisterous," "illeberal," and intimidating, Gorham submitted a report of the town's vote to the paper. He advised Otis "as a friend" that he should "divest himself of that obnoxious character" if he wanted to avoid "the vexing evil" of having mastiffs and curs bark at him. Unless he stopped being so obnoxious, his "high pretensions to exalted patriotism, will do him no honor" except in places where his "political conduct is happily less known" than it was in Barnstable. Barnstable thanked Gorham for setting the record straight and called Otis's protest "a wrong and Injurious Representation" of its position.

Bacon's warnings that "we should be more Tyrannized over by the People Here, our Neighbors than ever we was by Lord North," rang true as the Patriots tried to silence opposition, and as the Barnstable militia continued to divide between partisans of Otis and those of the Crockers. Bacon said he would "rather have a master Three Thousand miles off than here so near us." Gorham cautioned Bacon not to speak so freely, but Bacon felt obliged to discourage younger neighbors from fighting in a seemingly lost cause.

Bacon's warnings had more credibility as the war ground on, and Barnstable voters elected him to the Provincial Congress in 1778. Joseph Otis led a petition drive not to seat Bacon, as he was "an avowed Opposer of Congresses . . . & a professed Enemy to the Independency of America." Bacon organized a special Town Meeting to consider this. The meeting attributed Otis's petition, signed by twenty-nine people, to "an old family quarrel."

By chance, as the Provincial Congress prepared to decide whether to seat him, Bacon met Joseph Otis on the first floor of the State House (now called the Old State House) in Boston. The two men worked out an agreement. Otis would not object to seating Bacon; Bacon would resign and go back to Barnstable to work out the militia schism between Otis and the Crockers. Otis doubted that Bacon could do this, saying, "You can't Kill them Crockers Sam & Nell." Bacon knew he could not kill them, but he could "still them." In three weeks, Bacon said, he would "convince you all that I am a friend to my Country."

Bacon resigned; a special Town Meeting reelected him. Otis did not object. But Stephen Nye of Sandwich, one of the "body of the people" who had stopped the Barnstable court in 1774, said that Bacon's stubborn influence had kept Barnstable lukewarm to the cause of independence. Evidence against Bacon included a remarkable deposition from a mysterious Edward Davis, who claimed to be a spy. Davis charged Bacon with conspiring with other Cape Tories— Edward and Elisha Bourne of Sandwich, Doctor Fessenden of Harwich, and Captain Gideon Baty of Eastham—to support a British invasion of the Cape.

The Provincial Congress would not seat Bacon, but Barnstable voters elected him yet again in May. He went to Boston and told the Congress he was "a Tory but not an Enemy to his Country." He would not fight against the British, though "if they Landed & come to destroy his House, He did not know what he should do." The Congress rejected him again. Barnstable stubbornly refused to be represented by anyone else, reelecting the unseatable Bacon again in 1780.

The British did not come to destroy Bacon's house, but the British occupation of New York and Newport left Falmouth and the Elizabeth Islands vulnerable to attacks. Nantucket Sound and Buzzards Bay were under threat from both sides. Falmouth in 1777 sent a boat to Connecticut to buy corn, but a British privateer seized it. The captain escaped, made his way to

Falmouth, and alerted General Dimmick. Dimmick took twenty men in three whaleboats to wait at Tarpaulin Cove. When they saw the British privateer sailing with its prize toward Martha's Vineyard, they moved quickly. They boarded the prize and under British fire sailed to the west side of the Vineyard. The British pursued and drove them off the prize. Dimmick and his men regrouped, retook the vessel, and sailed with their load of corn to Woods Hole.

One evening Dimmick learned that two English privateers had taken an American schooner to Martha's Vineyard. Just before daybreak he and twenty-five men sailed for Edgartown, where they saw a British warship, the two privateers, and the schooner. They retook the schooner and took one of the privateers, sailing it and thirty-three prisoners across the sound to Osterville, on the Cape.

British raiders took 1,500 sheep from the Elizabeth Islands in 1778. The following April British foragers went ashore to raid farms at Woods Hole. A local Tory led them to the farms of Ephraim and Manasseh Swift, where they seized a dozen cattle. As they marched the cattle to the water, the Tory reported that Manasseh's wife made good cheese. The foragers decided to get it. Mrs. Swift was alone with her children when the raiding party knocked. She demanded to speak to their commander. She told him she presumed he was too much of a gentleman to molest a woman and children.

He asked about the cheese. Yes, she had cheese, but only enough for her family. He asked to buy some, and she told him that even if she had cheese to sell, she would not sell a crumb to him. With that the men marched to the dairy room. Stabbing wheels of cheese onto their bayonets, the soldiers turned to carry them off. But as they stepped past Mrs. Swift, she deftly slipped the stolen cheese from the bayonets into the folds of her apron, telling the British soldiers they were "a valiant set indeed—fit for two things—to rob hen roosts and make hen-pecked husbands."

Perhaps they should have robbed hen roosts. Back on the beach, their comrades had decided to kill the twelve cows, and then they could not get them onto the boats. This unsuccessful raid stung the British foragers. In retaliation for their failure to take either cattle or cheese, they decided to strike Falmouth. A party of naval officers stopped at the Loyalist John Slocum's Pasque Isle tavern. Slocum welcomed his king's men and their trade, but when he heard the talk of burning Falmouth, he had his son row to Woods Hole to alert Dimmick, whose men spent the night building fortifications. When ten British schooners and sloops appeared the next morning off the docks, Dimmick was waiting with two hundred Falmouth and Sandwich militiamen. The British did not land.

Despite the need to protect their homes from British raids, the towns of the Cape continued to send men to fight. Twenty-two men from Mashpee, Wampanoag Indians, enlisted; only one came back alive. From among the twenty-six houses north of Pond Village in Truro, twenty-eight men died in the war. Reverend Levi Whitman of Truro wrote, "No town suffered more during the war except those reduced to ashes."

All but deserted during the war, Truro and Provincetown made one of the Revolution's biggest captures. The British man-of-war *Somerset,* with its sixty-four guns that had blockaded Boston and bombarded

The 1779 alarm at Falmouth, painted by Franklin Lewis Gifford. (Courtesy Falmouth Historical Society)

Spencer Parry Kennard, HMS Somerset *on the Peaked Hill Bars,* 1978. The wreck occurred off Truro, November 1778. (Collection of the Town of Provincetown, courtesy Provincetown Art Commission)

Charlestown during the Battle of Bunker Hill, was caught in a gale on November 2, 1778, on Provincetown's back shore. It struck on the treacherous Peaked Hill bar, and the rushing tide pushed the vessel closer to the beach. Two hundred men drowned trying to reach the shore.

Four hundred eighty survivors made it, and Isaiah Atkins, a Truro selectman, accepted the *Somerset's* surrender. Colonel Enoch Hallett and the Yarmouth militia took charge of the survivors, who were marched in a grand parade to Boston. Joseph Otis and Barnstable's militia took charge of the wreck, which the people of Provincetown and Truro had already stripped. There was "wicked work at the wreck, and riotous doings," Otis observed. Truro men "took two-thirds and Provincetown one-third. There is a plundering gang that way."

If the story of David Snow and his young son, David, of Truro is not true, it should be. They missed the war entirely, though they were completely absorbed in it. They were fishing off Truro in 1775 when a British ship captured them. Accused of being rebels, they were taken first to Nova Scotia and then to England, where they were locked up in the Old Mill Prison near Plymouth. Their family in Truro presumed they had fallen off their boat, which was found floating in Cape Cod Bay.

But the Snows were not dead. The elder Snow during his years in prison was a model prisoner, and he organized a dance for the prisoners. As a band played and the prisoners stomped, Snow filed through the prison bars. He, his son, and thirty-four others escaped and made their way to the harbor. They found a scow, and they pushed out into the Channel. At daylight they were drifting off the coast. They spied a small sailing vessel, overpowered its crew, and sailed for France.

From Le Havre the Snows sailed in a ship bound for South Carolina, and from there they walked to Boston, where they took a boat to Provincetown. Little had changed in Truro. For seven years both had been given up for dead; Snow's wife fainted when he walked through his front door. Young David had been a boy when they disappeared; now he was a young man. He found a group of his peers, but he did not tell them who he was. One young lady said if he was not David Snow, he must be his ghost.

The Snows' story resembles that of Washington Irving's Rip Van Winkle, who slept through the Revolution and awoke in a world transformed. Truro, however, had not been transformed. Its people still farmed and fished. But the war had introduced Cape Codders to the rest of the world. After the war, Cape Codders would sign onto merchant and trading vessels that would take them to Oregon, China, Africa, and India, and they would pursue whales beyond their coastal waters into the southern Atlantic and the Pacific.

5

captains courageous

SLEEPY JOHN SEARS of Dennis knew that fishermen needed salt to preserve fish, and he knew the British controlled the salt supply. In 1776 Sears built a one-hundred-foot trough, ten feet wide, and covered it with removable shutters. Bucket by bucket, Sleepy John filled the trough with saltwater. Each day he opened the shutters, the sun evaporated the water, and at the end of the year he had eight bushels of salt.

Neighbors thought he was daft. But Sears bought the *Somerset*'s bilge pumps to fill his trough more quickly; he built a windmill to power the pumps. Out of sea and sun

The saltworks at Bass River, with a movable lid that could cover the evaporating water at night or in the rain; this was the Cape's last saltworks, which shut down in 1888. (Courtesy Chatham Historical Society)

Grand Banks fishermen landing a cod. The artist Griswald Tyng, born in Dorchester, painted in Orleans. (Collection of Mr. and Mrs. Thomas Davies)

Sears created one of the Cape's most important industries. By the 1830s, the Cape's 442 saltworks produced 669,064 bushels of salt every year, and the $2 million investment (equivalent to $28 million today) gave an annual return of 25 percent. For twenty miles south of Provincetown, John G. Palfrey said in 1839, the shore "seemed built of salt vats."

Salt made the Cape suddenly prosperous. With plenty of salt, Cape fishermen now had an advantage. The U.S. government went further and gave American fishermen a bounty. Fishing quickly became lucrative. Still, Cape Codders did not venture far from shore. They built traps for mackerel and other coastal fish, salting them down, drying them on flakes, or platforms, in their yards. Salted cod became a staple of the diet of

George Nickerson took this photograph of mackerel drying in a Provincetown yard. (Courtesy Historic New England)

slaves in the sugar islands of the Caribbean; and the cod was so important to the Massachusetts economy that a wooden one has hung in the State House of Representatives since the 1740s. Not to be outdone, the State Senate displays a mackerel.

The federal government also encouraged whaling, to meet the European demand for oil to light streets and lubricate machinery. Whaling had always been lucrative. Captain Jones had advised the Pilgrims that if they caught whales, they would pay off their debts in a year. The Pilgrims, though, were landsmen. The Indians hunted whales and kept lookouts on the high ground for whales close to shore, and the shout of "Towner!" meant that a whale had been sighted twice in the area. In their canoes the Indians would set out to force the whale ashore.

Oil so close to shore was too valuable to ignore. By the end of the seventeenth century, some Cape Codders were in the whaling business. According to English law, the king had rights to beached whales. The Plymouth authorities, defying the king's authority in most ways, believed they had inherited his cetacean prerogative. Finders of stray whales disagreed. By 1654 Plymouth compromised: if a whale was found within a mile of the beach, one barrel of its oil would go to market on Plymouth's account. This encouraged whalers to venture out more than a mile, but few Cape Codders were willing to do so. The English preferred to farm, not fish. Once the great supply of whales close to shore was gone, most residents returned their attention to raising corn and cattle. Whaling was a mainstay only in the rough settlement at Provincetown; in 1737 every Provincetown man could be found on one of twelve boats hunting whales off Greenland.

The British Parliamentarian Edmund Burke praised the enterprise of American whalers in 1775.

Look at the manner in which the people of New England have carried on their fishery. While we follow them among the tumbling mountains of ice, penetrating into the deepest recesses of Hudson's Bay; while we are looking for them beneath the arctic circle, we hear that they have pierced into the opposite region of polar cold—that they are at the antipodes, and engaged under the frozen Serpent of the South. Falkland Island, which seemed too remote and romantic an object for the grasp of natural ambition, is but a stage and resting place in the progress of their victorious industry. While some of them draw the line and strike the harpoon on the coast of Africa, others run the longitude and pursue the giant game along the shores of Brazil.

The Revolution disrupted whaling, but Secretary of State Thomas Jefferson focused the government's attention on American whalers. Thanks to Jefferson, whalers received a government bounty, and men from the Cape set out after the whales.

Fishing and whaling revived. But Britain had shut Americans out of its Caribbean ports. Americans could no longer sell their salted codfish in Jamaica or Barbados. Britain also encouraged Algiers to attack American ships, to keep Yankees from Spanish and Italian markets. But Americans were determined to find markets. (The American diplomat Joel Barlow commented that these Yankee captains would "sail into the mouth of hell" on the rumor the Devil was turning Catholic.)

With those markets closed, men sought other outlets for capital. Boston and New York investors bought two ships, the eighty-three-foot *Columbia* and the forty-foot sloop *Lady Washington,* and hired John Kendrick of Harwich (a part of Harwich that is now Orleans), a forty-seven-year-old former privateer captain, to command the *Columbia* and the expedition. Kendrick would buy furs from the Natives in the Pacific Northwest, trade them in China for tea and silver, and bring those goods home.

Chasing a whale.

The *Columbia* and *Lady Washington* sailed on October 1, 1787, and reached the Northwest early the following year. The members of the expedition bought otter and beaver pelts from the Indians. One story has Kendrick strapping two Native leaders to his cannon and threatening to shoot unless they agreed to his price. Captain Robert Gray, having switched vessels with Kendrick, sailed the *Columbia* to China that summer, stopping to name the Columbia River after his ship. Departing Canton, he continued around the world, bringing a cargo of Chinese tea into Boston. Kendrick sailed the *Lady Washington* to China in the fall, stopping in the Charlotte Islands and Hawai'i. After a year in Canton, trading furs for silver, tea,

Charles Hawthorne, *The Crew of the Philomena Manta,* 1915. (Collection of the Town of Provincetown, courtesy Provincetown Art Commission)

and silk, he sailed back to the Pacific Northwest, stopping briefly in Japan (the first American captain to show the flag there). He built himself a large house on Vancouver Island.

Kendrick set off for China again in 1791, by way of Hawai'i, and this time stayed in Canton for nine months. In the spring of 1793 he sailed back for Vancouver, and then sailed again for China. In Hawai'i in December 1794, he exchanged cannon salutes with a British

Cape Cod was isolated from the rest of the country, but not the world. Here, in the early twentieth century, is a Chinese man drying squid on a Chatham beach. (Courtesy Chatham Historical Society)

The *Lady Washington,* a replica built in 1989, is the official Tall Ship of the State of Washington. (Photo by Ron Arel; courtesy Grays Harbor Historical Seaport)

ship. The British sailors not only loaded their cannon, but they also took aim. What remained of Kendrick is buried in Hawai'i.

Kendrick had created a network of trade across the Pacific. He planted the American flag on the Pacific coast and carried it to China; by the middle of the nineteenth century the United States possessed California and Oregon; by the century's end the United States had Hawai'i and the Philippines. And in Canton, the only Chinese port open to foreigners before the 1850s, Americans were called "Boston men" because their ships had sailed from Boston, though most were navigated by Cape Codders.

The profits flowed back to Boston and were invested in the mills of Lowell and Lawrence, creating an American Industrial Revolution. Years later, Captain William Sturgis of Barnstable commented, "Were I required to select any particular event in the commercial history of our country to establish our reputation for bold enterprise and persevering energy in commercial pursuits, I should point to this expedition of the *Columbia* and *Washington.*"

Cape Codders discover the world: here Captain Robert Gray arrives at the Columbia River. (Courtesy Oregon State Capital, Eugene)

But trade did not expand smoothly. When the British and French threatened American commerce in the early nineteenth century, President Jefferson shut all American ports. No ships could enter or leave. The embargo erased many of the gains made since the Revolution and provoked resistance. Provincetown's frustrated customs official noted, "The mass of the population are interested in their [illegal contraband's] concealment and so far from giving assistance, threaten such opposition as renders the attempt . . . futile." The embargo did not keep the United States out of the European war.

President James Madison justified the War of 1812 as a way to protect free trade and sailors' rights. New Englanders supported free trade and sailors' rights, but they opposed the war. They blamed Madison and Jefferson for the disastrous embargo. Barnstable County held a Peace Convention, declaring that the war "originated in hatred to New England and to commerce" and in "subservience to the mandate of the Tyrant of France." Yarmouth vowed "not to engage in, encourage, or support it [the war] any further than we are compelled to do." Support for the war cost Congressman Isaiah Green of Barnstable his seat in 1812, though President Madison made him Barnstable collector of customs, the most important federal job on the Cape.

Nantucket made a truce with the British, allowing their fleet free use of the island, and, just as they had in 1776, the British used Provincetown as a base.

Some Cape Codders, though, served with distinction. Joshua Crosby of Orleans had served in the navy during the Tripolitan War

John "Mad Jack" Percival

OCCUPATION: Captain, U.S. Navy

LIFETIME: 1779–1862

HOMETOWN: Born in West Barnstable.

FAMILY: One of five children. Married Maria Pinkerton, c. 1809; no children; adopted niece Maria Weeks (b. 1825); took in nephew James Lawrence, sister's son, 1828; adopted nephew James Percival, brother's son, 1839; during 1826 visit to Honolulu "married" Native woman.

"Mad Jack" Percival. Courtesy of the U.S.S. *Constitution* Museum.

CAREER: Captured British sloop *Eagle* off Sandy Hook, July 1813. As lieutenant in command of *Dolphin,* was first American naval officer to visit Honolulu, 1826; provoked and quelled riot of sailors over missionary ban on women visiting ships; forced Hawaiian government to lift ban. Destroyer fleet in Pearl Harbor still observes "Mad Jack Percival Day" every May 11. Commanded USS *Constitution* on world cruise, 1844–46; in Da Nang, Vietnam, led naval battle that failed to force local government to free French missionaries held hostage.

"I have lived to find that a fair share of patriotism and bravery, with a full share of zeal and integrity in the execution of my duties as a Navy officer, are insufficient securities for an equal share of actual employment when brought in conflict with sectional and political prejudice."

(1801–5) and was aboard the U.S.S. *Constitution,* manning one of the guns during *Constitution*'s half-hour battle off Nova Scotia in August 1812 with the British frigate *Guerrière,* in which the wooden-hulled *Constitution* earned the nickname "Old Ironsides" for the way cannonballs bounced harmlessly off its sides while gun crews like Crosby's destroyed the *Guerrière.*

His family had this portrait of Alfred Nye Crosby made before he went to sea; he never returned. (Courtesy Chatham Historical Society)

Other Cape men served aboard privateers, private ships licensed to attack enemy vessels. Crews and captain shared in the profits of captures. Prizes taken south of the Cape would be run into Hyannis Harbor, unloaded, the vessels sold, and the cargoes carted to Barnstable and shipped to Boston. Other merchant captains ran the blockade. Captain Daniel Bacon of Barnstable, son of Edward Bacon, slipped six tons of goods through the British blockade of Americans in Canton.

As they had been in the Revolution, Cape towns were exposed to British attacks. In early 1814 two British vessels came into Tarpaulin Cove to attack Falmouth. According to local tradition, John Slocum again warned the town, and eighty-one-year-old Joseph Dimmick came to the front of the militia. His house became a refuge for women and children.

As the British shelled Falmouth, Ichabod Hatch sat defiantly in his ruined doorway, shouting, "There, Damn ye, John Bull, see if ye can do that again!" He moved when another shot hit above his head. Ann Freeman fortunately was out of bed when a British cannonball hit it, sending feathers flying through the house. Already annoyed that the blockade had ruined his shipping business, Elijah Swift was furious when a British shot destroyed his dining room sideboard. When the British vessels pulled out at sundown, Swift began building a fifty-ton schooner in his yard. He launched this privateer by year's end, christening it *Status Ante Bellum*.

The British privateer *Retaliation* came to harass the Cape in October. Weston Jenkins stowed thirty-one men on his sloop *The Two Friends*. Captain Porter of the *Retaliation*, seeing the apparently unarmed merchant sloop, fired a warning shot. Jenkins, on deck with one sailor, feigned surrender. Porter and five sailors rowed over to claim the prize, but when they reached it twenty-nine armed men suddenly stood at the rail. Porter drew his pistol. Jenkins warned, "One more move and I'll send you all to the bottom."

Jenkins took the prisoners aboard. Quietly he had *The Two Friends* rowed back to the *Retaliation,* whose crew still thought it had surrendered. Now they surrendered to Jenkins without a fight. "That Yankee captain played me a damn sharp trick," Captain Porter told a Falmouth man he met many years later, "but he treated me like a gentleman."

Repulsed at Falmouth, the British turned their attention to other parts of the Cape. Captain Richard Raggett of the fifty-gun warship H.M.S. *Spencer,* based at Provincetown, notified each Cape town that he would destroy its saltworks unless it paid him a ransom. Brewster paid $4,000, and Eastham $1,000. Orleans and Barnstable refused.

From Maine, Matthew Cobb wrote to his brother Daniel in Barnstable, "I hope you will not purchase your safety, for that would be very degrading indeed." He wrote that the British "cannot injure you with their ships. If they land their sailors to destroy your houses you can with a litle spirit that may be got up, drive them into the sea." It took "a litle spirit," but Barnstable showed it. Tradition has it that on a Sunday morning the alarm spread that the British had landed at

Captain Richard Raggett of the *Spencer* tells the selectmen and salt makers of Orleans to give him the "moderate sum" of $1,000 (equivalent to about $8,000 today) or he will destroy their saltworks. They declined the offer. (Courtesy Orleans Historical Society)

Charles Hawthorne, *The Widow*, 1917. Waiting for a boat that will never return, this widow stands with her orphaned infant on the Provincetown dock. (Huntington Museum of Art, Huntington, W.V.)

Scorton Neck; within two minutes the church was empty and the militia out. The British did not come into Barnstable Harbor. Not content with the militia, Isaiah Green brought four cannon by oxcart from Boston. The British did not try another landing.

The Revolutionary veteran Isaac Snow drilled the Orleans militia. (Remembering how well the French in Orléans had treated him during the Revolution, when he had taken a respite from privateering, Snow had suggested this as a name for their town when it broke off from Eastham in 1797.) On December 9, 1814, Captain Frederick Marryat on the *Newcastle* shelled the Orleans village at Rock Harbor. A landing party came ashore, burning two fishing boats and seizing a schooner, which they sailed to Provincetown. But the Orleans militia came out, driving back the British, killing one soldier and sinking one of their whaleboats. They drove the British from Orleans, and no enemy would again attack the Cape for a hundred years.

As the Orleans militia fought off the British invasion, American and British diplomats worked out a treaty, which they signed late in December (news did not reach the United States until February 1815). The peace opened the world to American ships and American traders. The men who had served on privateers served after the war on the merchant ships that carried American goods to the rest of the world.

Long voyages in pursuit of whales and markets brought hardships, not the least of which were scurvy and other diseases from which sailors suffered. The British had discovered that lime juice prevented scurvy. The United States did not produce citrus crops, and the British were reluctant to provide maritime competitors with easy cures. But cranberries grew on Cape Cod, and though no one at the time knew there was such a thing as vitamin C, that a lack of it brought on scurvy, and that cranberries and limes both contained vitamin C, Cape Codders saw a connection between the cranberry and healthier sailors. Cape Cod captains took barrels of cranberries on their voyages.

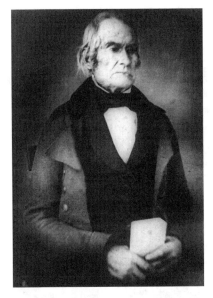

Isaac Snow, a Revolutionary war veteran, suggested naming Eastham's southern parish Orleans. (Courtesy Orleans Historical Society)

The September 1815 hurricane covered Captain Henry Hall's Dennis bog in sand. He thought he had harvested his last cranberry. But instead of dying, the plants were stronger and more fruitful in 1816. It was not a fluke. Hall experimented and found that the sand helped the berries grow. With the chance aid of the hurricane, Hall found a way to boost production as a growing fleet and longer voyages increased demand for cranberries.

The sea, with its salt, fish, whales, and trade routes, brought

Cape Cod an unprecedented half century of prosperity. But it was not ostentatious prosperity. An 1864 visitor wrote, "The inhabitants of this ridge of drift sand are remarkably thrifty. One sees nowhere indications of extreme destitution. But while most of the people are independent in their circumstances, there is not much wealth, and no show of it." Cape Codders prospered, but their barren land and the relentless economy required by ocean voyages constrained their ostentation.

That prosperity did not last. Merchant captains were likely to move to Boston, and their children would go to work for the capitalists who hired their fathers. There was little opportunity on the barren peninsula, so the Cape's children moved on to Boston, New York, or farther. The Cape's population reached 35,990 in 1860, and then declined. It would not be that high again until World War II.

Cape Codders sought opportunities elsewhere. Shipping and whaling by their nature created mobility. When the whaler *Independence* foundered off the Hawaiian Islands in 1821, Joseph Young made it to shore. He married the daughter of Kamehameha III and became the premier, and his grandson became King Kalaukaua.

A West Harwich captain invited to dinner in Hong Kong by an English merchant was promised "a New England dinner." It turned

The cranberry harvest—the lines keep the women on the straight path through the bog. (Courtesy Massachusetts Historical Society)

out his hostess was from East Dennis, daughter of a merchant who had sailed to Hong Kong, where she met and married the Englishman. Strange indeed that an East Dennis woman and a West Harwich man met in Hong Kong rather than at home, where their paths would have frequently crisscrossed.

Mrs. Cordelia Childs of Falmouth was the first American woman to visit Japan, though she did so illegally. Foreigners had been barred from Japan in the 1600s. But whalers such as her husband touched surreptitiously at ports beyond the shogun's control. Nine years after Mrs. Childs visited Hondo, the U.S. government, responding to the needs of the whaling fleet, forced Japan to open its ports to foreigners. Japan did so, and it also reformed its economic and political system, becoming an industrial power and a constitutional monarchy. A British officer visiting in 1863 thought the Japanese stared because they had never seen a Westerner. But stopping in a shop advertising "Ship's Stores," he met the proprietor, from Hyannis.

Robert Bennett Forbes said he "would not be at all surprised if, when the North Pole is discovered, a Cape Cod man will be found there fishing." He was not far off the mark. When Donald Baxter MacMillan was nine, his father was lost off the Grand Banks; his mother took in washing until she died in poverty. Sent from the family home in Provincetown to Maine, he worked his way through Bowdoin College, then taught at a prep school and in a wilderness camp fostering self-reliance. Captain Robert Peary invited MacMillan to join his 1908–9 expedition to the North Pole. This began MacMillan's lifelong career in polar exploration. He studied Eskimos and their Arctic environment and mapped the coasts of Labrador, Greenland, and Ellesmere Island.

Not all had to venture so far from home. David Snow of Orleans went to Boston, where he became the owner of most of that prosperous city's maritime wharves. Snow was a devout Methodist, and when his business partner, Isaac Rich, founded a Methodist school, which eventually became Boston University, Snow was a significant contributor.

Caleb Chase, the youngest of seventeen children in a Harwich family, did not follow his brothers to sea, but he managed their trade, and went into business with Charles Sanborn. Though they handled many

Lorenzo Dow Baker

OCCUPATION: Merchant trader

LIFETIME: 1840–1908

HOMETOWN: Born in Wellfleet.

FAMILY: Son of a Wellfleet fisherman. Married Martha Hopkins, 1861; sons Lorenzo D., Joshua Hamblen, and Reuben Rich, daughter Martha.

ACCOMPLISHMENTS: Brought first cargo of bananas from Jamaica to Boston; expanded this banana trade into founding of United Fruit. Built luxury winter resort Titchfield Hotel at Port Antonio, Jamaica, and Chequessett Inn, a summer resort, on Wellfleet's Mercantile Wharf. Considered father of Jamaican tourism.

Lorenzo Dow Baker. (Courtesy Boston Public Library)

The archbishop of the West Indies said of Baker in 1905: "We admire and honor Capt. Baker for his character and religious devotion. In his career we have seen his high moral virtues and a kindly philanthropy associated with absorbing interest in public responsibilities and great capacity and success in business, and instead of being starved and dwarfed by this association, these virtues have been made capable of ministering more effectively to the general welfare."

items, eventually they found their niche in the coffee trade, under the name Chase & Sanborn.

An Eastham butcher, Gustavus Franklin Swift, went west to Chicago in 1875 and revolutionized the American meatpacking industry. Swift shifted the meatpackers from salt to refrigeration, so Chicago could ship fresh meat east. A massive advertising campaign convinced Americans that Swift's fresh beef was healthful. In Chicago's slaughterhouses Swift developed a conveyor-belt system for the more efficient slaughter and butchering of cattle, a gruesome process that inspired Henry Ford in the auto industry and repulsed the socialist writer Upton Sinclair to such a degree that he wrote *The Jungle*.

Lorenzo Dow Baker of Wellfleet was in the Caribbean lumber trade, bringing tropical lumber to New England. In Jamaica Baker became intrigued with bananas. He learned how to ship the fruit so it would be ripe when it reached the markets. The company became United Fruit. Baker also built a luxury resort in Jamaica, opening the winter tourist trade to that island; in Wellfleet he bought an old wharf and created the Chequessett Inn, a summer resort staffed with Jamaicans. The Jamaican government honored him for his contributions to their economy.

Men like Snow, Chase, Swift, and Baker found their fortunes elsewhere as the brief period of Cape prosperity was ending. Discoveries of salt deposits in New York made Cape Cod's saltworks obsolete. Within a year or two all were dismantled, their timbers used for houses or barns. The first petroleum well in Pennsylvania in 1859 (the product of which would surpass whale oil in many uses) and Confederate privateers during the Civil War wiped out the whaling fleet, though stubborn Provincetowners chased whales into the 1920s.

With so many men at sea, the women at home went to work in small factories. But this industrial economy succumbed to competition from larger enterprises closer to labor sources and markets. Brewster's factory village, producing woolen textiles, could not compete with the larger industries in Lowell or New Bedford. Sandwich's glassworks flourished until 1888, then disappeared when the workers went on strike for higher wages. Instead of accommodating the strikers, the owners shut down the factory.

Lorenzo Dow Baker built the Chequessett Inn, a luxury resort, on an old fishing pier in Wellfleet.

The Boston and Sandwich Glass Works. (Courtesy Boston Athenaeum)

Sandwich, with the smoke of the glassworks billowing overhead.

The Cape's population shrank, but it also changed. The Nickersons, Chases, and Paines moved out, replaced by Santos, Silvas, and Cabrals. Whalers, always short of men, picked up crews in the Azores and Cape Verde Islands. There seemed to be better fishing off the Cape, and better opportunities in the dying Cape industries, than on the Portuguese islands. These immigrants found cheap housing and ready access to fishing grounds. From the Azores and Cape Verde Islands came the first Portuguese, who by the end of the nineteenth century had formed a vital part of the Provincetown community.

Into the late nineteenth century, small factories thrived on the Cape, using the labor of underemployed Cape women and children too young for the sea.

After the Provincetown saltworks folded, Nickerson's Whale and Menhaden Oil Works continued to extract fish oil at Herring Cove, not far from Race Point Light. There was still a living to be made from the sea, and Provincetown men kept hunting whales for their flexible baleen, used in umbrellas and corsets, and ambergris, a malodorous waxy substance found in the intestines of diseased whales. Ambergris is used in perfume; only a ton of it came on the market in the nineteenth century, and most of that was sold by David Stull of Provincetown. The going rate was $500 a pound.

Nathaniel Atwood stayed on in Provincetown after his father closed his Long Point saltworks. Atwood was a fisherman. He studied fish and by 1852 knew more about fish than anyone else in the

Marine Biological Laboratory's research vessel *Vigilant* returns from its last cruise of the season in August 1897. The young woman at right in the stern is Gertrude Stein. (Photograph by Baldwin Coolidge; courtesy Historic New England)

Commonwealth. Louis Agassiz, the country's leading scientist, called on Atwood in 1852, and five years later Henry David Thoreau came to talk fish with Atwood, who was elected to the American Academy of Arts and Sciences. His knowledge of fish earned him election to that assemblage, but his good sense won him election to the State House of Representatives. The House doorkeeper thought it was not becoming to have a member of that august body listed as a "fisherman," so he listed Atwood as a "master mariner."

Fishing declined, but the study of fish increased. In 1888 seventeen scientists formed the Marine Biological Laboratory in Woods Hole, one of the premier biological labs in the world. Fifty-six of its students, researchers, teachers, or members have received the Nobel Prize. In the 1930s Dr. Frederick Hammett opened a Marine Experimental Station in Truro, studying sea life to understand the nature of cancer. And in 1930 scientists launched the Woods Hole Oceanographic Institute to study the oceans and their interactions with the Earth's systems. Fishermen and mariners used the oceans to make a living; once many fish were gone and sailing vessels became obsolete, scientists turned to the ocean to understand the world. ⌐

on old cape cod

SOLOMON ATTAQUIN went to sea at age twelve, cooking on a Grand Banks fishing schooner. He retired in 1840 as captain of a coasting vessel. Returning to his native Mashpee, Attaquin opened a hotel for sportsmen, following a custom of his Wampanoag people, who had hosted guests since Gosnold arrived. Successful men from Boston and New York, statesmen like Daniel Webster and Grover Cleveland, came to Attaquin's inn to hunt and fish in Mashpee's woods and ponds, an undeveloped area close to the urban and industrial centers of the United States.

Solomon Attaquin's inn at Mashpee. (Courtesy Massachusetts Historical Society)

The Mashpees had fought hard to keep their woods. After the Revolution the legislature appointed guardians for the Indian community. One of them, the Harvard-trained minister Phineas Fish, was more interested in the Mashpees' timber than the Mashpees' souls. In 1833 the Mashpees protested against Fish and the guardians, and on July 4 of that year the Reverend William Apess, a Pequot serving as minister to the Mashpees, was arrested for blocking white men from cutting Mashpee lumber. "We as a tribe, will rule our selves," the Mashpees insisted, "and have the right so to do for all men are born free and Equal says the Constitution of the Country." The legislature acceded to Mashpee's insistence that it had as much right to govern itself as did Falmouth or Barnstable; the Mashpees promptly dismissed Fish from their meetinghouse.

There was less pressure on land in Mashpee as the nineteenth century progressed, as the Cape's industries and its population both disappeared. The nation grew, but the Cape shrank. By the end of World War I there were three times as many Americans as there had been when the Civil War began; the Cape population was only three-quarters what it had been. Nature reclaimed the Cape's factories and processing plants. On the Cape, as Henry David Thoreau had said, all man's works are wrecks. A closed mill or factory was no different from a beached vessel. What the neighbors would not strip, nature would erase.

President Cleveland was delighted that his Buzzards Bay neighbors were "independent, not obtrusively curious, and I only have to behave myself and pay my taxes to be treated like any other citizen of the

Solomon Attaquin

OCCUPATION: Hotelier and shipowner

LIFETIME: 1810–95

HOMETOWN: Born in Mashpee.

FAMILY: Married Cynthia Conant; daughters Melissa (1838–77), Nancy (1856–62).

CAREER: After going to sea as a cook, and rising to be a captain and shipowner, opened Hotel Attaquin in 1840. Guests included Daniel Webster, Henry David Thoreau, and Grover Cleveland. Continued to work on coastal vessels between Boston and Albany. Mashpee selectman, 1837–52, and afterward; town clerk, several years in 1840 and 1860s; first postmaster of Mashpee, 1871–89.

At a legislative hearing, February 1869, about whether Mashpee should become a town immediately, and individual Indians have rights as citizens, including the rights to vote and sell property:

Solomon Attaquin. (Courtesy David Kew, capecodhistory.us)

"[If the legislature delays, by the time Mashpees have rights] I shall be gone, and all the rest that have spoken here, and we shall not see the day that we shall be free men—men that have all the rights and privileges of citizens of the Common-wealth and the United States. I want to see that day come before my head is covered up. I want to see the day that I am a citizen and man, as well as other men, and I say we are ready for it today."

United States." He was fond of the story about getting lost in the dark woods after a day of fishing. Disoriented by a sudden downpour, he spent hours tramping through the rain before he saw a farmhouse light. He knocked on the door. From an upstairs window—"What do you want?"

"This is the president, " Cleveland answered. "I'm lost, and I'd like to stay here tonight."

"Well, stay there." The window shut.

The peaceful Mashpee pond where an actor, Joe Jefferson, and President Grover Cleveland fished in solitude. (Courtesy Massachusetts Historical Society)

Men like Webster and Cleveland came to get away from fashionable society, to fish or to hunt in the Cape's ponds or woods. A fishing companion in Mashpee recalled Webster gazing at the trees across the pond, ignoring his line slack in the water. Webster's heart and mind, he thought, were not on fishing. He was right. Webster "seemed to be gazing at the overhanging trees, and presently advancing one foot and extending his right hand commenced to speak, 'Venerable Men! You have come down to us from a former generation,'" rehearsing the oration he would give at the dedication of the Bunker Hill Monument in 1825.

A man and his dog escape from the city to hunt ducks in the quiet waters of Orleans. (Photograph by Henry L. Hadcock; courtesy Historic New England)

Cape Cod offered a spiritual solace missing elsewhere. Methodists gathered in Wellfleet in August 1819 for a camp-meeting revival, and every summer thereafter attendees came for a week of prayer, camping in tents and sharing meals. The revivals moved in 1828 to Eastham, to a place the Methodists called Millennium Grove. Seeing "the heaps of clam-shells left under the tables" at Millennium Grove, Thoreau thought the "camp-meeting must be a singular combination of prayer-meeting and picnic."

Thoreau thought the widows and orphans of its fishermen made the Cape receptive to revivals. Fifty-seven Truro men died in the October gale of 1841, which also killed twenty-eight men from Dennis. But the attendees were not just the Cape's widows. Nearly seven thousand Methodists poured off the trains when the revivals moved to Yarmouth in 1863, spending a week singing, preaching, and eating chowder and sandwiches. The Yarmouth revivalists replaced their tents with cottages and cabins.

The Eastham Camp Meetings were a combination spiritual revival and community reunion. (Courtesy Library of Congress)

Visitors arriving at the Eastham Camp Meeting by sloop disembarked onto a carriage, hoping not to get their feet wet. (Courtesy Library of Congress)

The Reverend Elisha Perry, a Rhode Island preacher born in Centerville, invited twenty-four ministers in 1872 to vacation on his family's Strawberry Hill land. The working vacation began with a 5:00 A.M. prayer meeting and proved so successful that the ministers returned, bought beachfront property, and named their community Craigville to honor the Christian Bible Institute's Dr. J. Austin Craig. Captain Dennis Sturgis built a hotel, and the ministers opened bathhouses and offered other amenities.

Sportsmen and revivalists were the first tourists. Neither wanted to change the land they found. Thoreau predicted in 1857 that the "time must come when this coast will be a place of resort," though he did not think it would ever be agreeable to "the fashionable world," which preferred the elegance of Newport or the Victorian resorts of Long Branch or Cape May. The rustic Cape would not suit vacationers who wanted "a ten-pin alley, or a circular railway, or an ocean of mint-julep." Those who sought "more of the wine than the brine," Thoreau said, "will be disappointed here."

Harvard's President A. Lawrence Lowell, writing in the 1930s, thought the first summer visitors in the years after the Civil War "were very different from the summer visitors of the present day." The

Lowells stayed in the old family homestead at Cotuit, drawn by inexpensive (if not free) accommodations, enjoying the extended leisure the academic calendar afforded. Lowell said that his family and others of the early summer visitors "stayed much longer and interested themselves in the local life" more deeply than subsequent visitors, and "they did not absorb or change the occupation of the people." Cape Cod was different from home, the people who lived there were different. The Lowells recognized that this community in Cotuit would continue when they and other visitors were back in Boston.

Sons and daughters of the Cape who left for better opportunities began to come back as visitors. When Falmouth's Congregational minister died, his widow and his daughter, Katharine Lee Bates, left for Wellesley, where Katharine would spend the rest of her life as a professor, returning each summer to Falmouth. Bates is best known for verses she wrote after a hiking up Pike's Peak, about the "purple mountain majesty above the fruited plain." The second verse recalls "Pilgrim feet" blazing "a thoroughfare for freedom . . . across the wilderness." Bates's ode to "Falmouth by the Sea" celebrates the town church bell, cast a century earlier by Paul Revere. She hoped the "Living voice of Paul Revere," ringing out in Falmouth, would "Let the future not forget / What the past accounted dear!"

Like Bates, Thornton Burgess of Sandwich lost his father at a young age. He worked on a farm to support the family, then moved to Springfield. After he lost his wife, he wrote bedtime stories for his young son, drawing on the natural world of his Cape Cod boyhood. For fifty years Burgess's weekly column, 15,000 stories, and 170 books chronicled the adventures of Reddy Fox, Jimmy Skunk, Grandfather Frog, and Peter Rabbit in their Briar Patch. He was for half a century the country's most beloved author, and for all time the Cape's most prolific; Burgess's stories awakened a sensitivity to the natural world in his young readers. After his death his home in western Massachusetts became an Audubon sanctuary, his Sandwich home was organized as a museum devoted to his life and works, and the farm he worked as a boy became the Thornton Burgess Nature Center. What other author is memorialized in three museums? Is there another so worthy?

No one did more to promote the Cape as a place of unique characters and communities than the novelist Joseph Lincoln. Born in

Katharine Lee Bates

OCCUPATION: Literature professor, Wellesley College; poet

LIFETIME: 1859–1929

HOMETOWN: Born in Falmouth.

FAMILY: Youngest of five children of Falmouth's Congregational minister; father died when she was an infant. Lifetime committed partnership with Katharine Coman, professor of economics and dean at Wellesley.

ACCOMPLISHMENTS: Professor and chair of Wellesley's English Department; founder of New England Poetry Club; active in labor reform and the New England Settlements Movement.

Katharine Lee Bates. (Courtesy Falmouth Historical Society)

> . . . *down the curve of our wind-obeying cape,*
> *The low, white, drifted dunes are wavy like the sea.*
> *Early our thoughts were molded to the unconscious shape*
> *Of immortality.*
>
> *There is many a shrine for pilgrims—the fountain*
> *that quenched our thirst,*
> *The hard-scaled summit of vision, the field of our*
> *perilous strife,*
> *But holy the awe that broodeth o'er the spot where we*
> *tasted first*
> *The sacrament of life.*

Brewster, Lincoln was living in New Jersey and working as a copywriter in New York in 1903 when he decided to write a novel in his spare time. *Cap'n Eri*, set in a fictional Cape Cod town, sold so well that every year for the next forty Lincoln wrote a similar book. A

Thornton W. Burgess

OCCUPATION: Writer; creator of the *Tales of Peter Rabbit*

LIFETIME: 1874–1965

HOMETOWN: Born and spent childhood years in Sandwich.

FAMILY: Father died when his son was an infant. Married Nina Osborne, 1905; one son; Nina died following year. Married Fannie P. Johnson, 1911; two stepsons.

ACCOMPLISHMENTS: Author of more than 170 books and 15,000 stories for children, which promoted conservation and the environment, syndicated daily in American newspapers from 1912 to 1960; received gold medal from Boston Museum of Science for "leading children down the path to the wide wonderful world of the outdoors."

Thornton W. Burgess visits third-graders in his hometown of Sandwich, 1951. (Courtesy Boston Public Library)

"It has been said that Cape Codders by birth rather than by adoption have salt in their hair, sand between their toes, and herring blood in their veins. Of these they never wholly rid themselves, nor do they want to. . . . Those who have spent the greater part of their lives far from the Cape must return to it at intervals. They must. It is the homing urge of the herring. . . . Others may boast of their ancestry but the pride of the born Cape Codder is the land of his birth."

smooth and entertaining writer, Lincoln spun out simple plots. The seemingly naive locals of Harniss or Wellmouth constantly undermined schemes of sharp-minded outsiders who sought to build chain stores or resorts in their tradition-bound communities. By 1927 five of

Lincoln's books had been made into films, and with his royalties he built a Chatham summer home, which itself became a tourist attraction. Visitors flocked to see Lincoln's house and the world he created. Chester Crocker, a year-round resident, remarked, "We Cape Codders have to read Joe's books to find out how to act, so we won't disappoint the summer folks."

Summer folks became a mainstay of the Cape economy. Nostalgia helped bring them in. Sandwich organized the first "Old Home Week" in 1902, to bring is displaced children and grandchildren back to visit. Harwich followed in 1903, and Centerville in 1905. Cape descendants throughout the country were called back to Cape Cod. The industrializing and urbanizing nation was experiencing at this time a Colonial revival. Americans, after a cataclysmic Civil War, labor strife and Indian wars in the 1870s and 1880s, and a major depression in the 1890s, yearned for a simpler past. Thanksgiving, established as a holiday during the Civil War, focused attention on the Pilgrims' world.

Seeing the success of the Cape's Old Home Weeks, Boston held one in 1907. As part of the festivities, the tea magnate Sir Thomas Lipton sponsored a race of Grand Banks fishing schooners. Men and boats from Boston, Gloucester, and Cape Cod competed. Captain Marion Perry of Provincetown's *Rose Dorothea* brought home the Lipton Cup.

Provincetown was still celebrating two weeks later, on August 20, 1907, when President Theodore Roosevelt arrived to dedicate the Pilgrim Monument. Eight battleships fired salutes as Roosevelt stepped off the yacht *Mayflower,* welcomed by Governor Curtis Guild, the British ambassador, and Senator Henry Cabot Lodge. Plans to commemorate the Pilgrims had been made as early as 1852, but nothing had been done other than placing a plaque in Provincetown Town Hall. Both Town Hall and the plaque burned in 1877. Boston's Cape Cod Association, descendants of Cape residents living in Boston, revived the idea of a Pilgrim monument, and in 1892 they formed the Cape Cod Memorial Association of Provincetown. Brewster's Pilgrim Club joined representatives from other Cape towns to ensure the proper telling of the Pilgrims' history on the Cape.

Joseph C. Lincoln

OCCUPATION: Novelist

LIFETIME: 1870–1944

HOMETOWN: Born in Brewster; built summer home in Chatham.

FAMILY: Father died in Charleston, South Carolina, 1871. Married Florence Sargent, 1897; one son.

ACCOMPLISHMENTS: After success with first book, *Cape Cod Ballads* (1902), gave up career as publicist for bankers to write novels on Cape Cod town life; wrote more than forty, several of which were made into motion pictures.

Joseph C. Lincoln, sitting on a stone wall, with the Chatham windmill in the background. (Courtesy Chatham Historical Society)

"My father was a sea captain, and so was his father, and his father before him, and all my uncles. My mother's people followed the sea. I suppose that if I had been born a few years earlier, I would have had my own ship."

They proposed a granite tower, 252 feet 7 inches tall, on High Pole Hill, to "be seen from every town on Cape Cod" and by "every vessel coming in or going out of Massachusetts Bay." The association's president, J. Henry Sears of Brewster, thought the tower would be "an excellent object lesson" to the tens of thousands of immigrants "coming into the country." Henry Baker of Hyannis observed, "Every incoming foreign steamer, bringing immigrants to our shores, when it sails into Boston harbor will pass that monument. What an object lesson it will be to him!"

Stones for the monument came from throughout the country, donated by Mayflower Societies. The church in Yorkshire, England, where William Bradford had been baptized sent a stone, carried

President Theodore Roosevelt lays the Pilgrim Monument cornerstone, Provincetown, 1907.

across the Atlantic free of charge by the Cunard Line, which brought many immigrants to America. Stones arrived from the Dutch churches where the Pilgrims had worshipped, and the Eastham doorstep of Plymouth's Governor Prence was put at the entryway. Three years later President William Howard Taft came to dedicate the Pilgrim Monument, still one of the most frequently visited sites on Cape Cod.

The moon illuminates the Pilgrim Monument, the steeples of Provincetown, and the harbor. (Courtesy of the artist, Robert Clibbon)

An art class on the beach in Provincetown.

By this time Provincetown, once one of the Commonwealth's richest communities, was an isolated fishing village. Petroleum and the Civil War had killed the whaling fleet, and steam engines made clipper ships obsolete. The midcentury wharves were crumbling. Fishing remained, and the Portuguese had replaced Yankees in the Grand Banks sailboats and dories.

Charles W. Hawthorne, son of a Maine sea captain, came to Provincetown in 1899, not to fish but to paint. Hawthorne had studied painting in New York, and he found Provincetown's unique light, color, and residents fascinating. Living in the town was cheap, and struggling fishermen, their wives, and their widows had rooms and fishing sheds to rent. Hawthorne opened the Cape Cod School of Art, holding classes outside to take advantage not of the scenery, but of the light. Artists were not to paint "pretty pictures" but to focus on color, on how things fit together. Painting, said Hawthorne, was "putting one spot of color next to another." Anyone could find beauty in something beautiful, Hawthorne said, but a true artist could find beauty in a freight depot or a rusted can on the beach.

Charles Hawthorne, *Fish Cleaners.* Hawthorne taught his students that real art was finding beauty where they did not expect it, such as in men cleaning fish. (Collection of the Town of Provincetown, courtesy Provincetown Art Commission)

Hawthorne's dynamic personality attracted other artists, also seeking the essence of color and form, to Provincetown. The war in Europe brought artists who might otherwise have gone to France, and in 1914 they formed the Provincetown Art Association. Sixty artists showed their work in Provincetown's Town Hall the next year. By 1921 they had built a museum. Every year since the Art Association has exhibited new work by members.

Commercial Street, Provincetown, early 1930s, with the bus approaching. (Courtesy Boston Public Library)

This was a period of transition in American art, to modernism and abstraction. The modernist Ross Moffett, a Hawthorne student who settled in Provincetown, noted that all art is an abstraction, but some traditionalists thought the modernists were becoming too abstract. After the artists John Whorf and Richard Miller embarrassed the Art Association by submitting a mock-cubist painting by the fictional artist Ad Wolgast (the real name of an old prizefighter), the Art Association held separate shows for modernists and traditionalists. By the end of the 1930s, though, all were exhibited together again.

Writers followed the artists. Mary Heaton Vorse, the foremost writer on the American labor movement, came in the 1910s and stayed until her death in 1966. Susan Glaspell and her husband, the theater director George Cram Cook, settled in Provincetown's East End. One of the century's best-selling authors, Glaspell wrote nine novels and four plays and received the Pulitzer Prize for *Alison's House,* a play based on the life of Emily Dickinson. Glaspell and Cook in 1915 formed the Provincetown Players, an experimental theater group that

Eugene O'Neill, his son Shane, and his wife Agnes Boulton O'Neill, outside their home at the former Peaked Hill Life-Saving Station. (Courtesy Shaeffer-O'Neill Collection, Charles E. Shain Library, Connecticut College, New London, Conn.)

performed plays on Mary Vorse's wharf. Just as Hawthorne rejected painting as mere decoration, the Provincetown Players rejected theater as entertainment.

Fortunately for actors and audiences, Eugene O'Neill arrived in 1916. The son of an actor and theater impresario, O'Neill came with a knapsack filled with plays. The reception given his first one, *Bound East for Cardiff,* inspired the Players to move to Greenwich Village, and it inspired O'Neill to stay in Provincetown. He and his wife Agnes Boulton O'Neill remained for nine years, mostly in the old Peaked Hill Bars Life-Saving Station his parents gave them as a wedding gift.

The Life-Saving Station had been converted into a living space by the New York literary socialite Mabel Dodge, who had left Provincetown in 1919 to start an artists' colony in Taos, New Mexico. "Hard to get to and get out of," O'Neill wrote of the Life-Saving Station, "but a grand place to be alone and undisturbed when you want to work." When he learned that his play *Beyond the Horizon* had won the Pulitzer Prize in 1920, O'Neill ran to the beach and dove into the Atlantic surf. After the O'Neills moved out, the shore beneath the station eroded and the house fell into the sea.

One of O'Neill's walks through the dunes aroused suspicions among locals, who reported two young strangers, possibly German spies, carrying a black box. Police officers found O'Neill, the artist Charles Demuth, and O'Neill's typewriter. Fear of German spies was not entirely fanciful. One Sunday morning in July 1918 Captain Joe Perry of Provincetown was in a coal barge convoy off Orleans. He, his wife, daughter, and crew were having their sausage and eggs when they heard two sharp booms. Going to the deck, Perry saw a German U-boat half a mile away. He hurried his family and crew into their dory, and they rowed away as their barge sank.

A crowd gathered on the Orleans shore as a lone plane from the Chatham Air Station came to defend the barges. (According to tradition, most of the men from Chatham Air Station were at a baseball

Eugene O'Neill celebrates winning the Pulitzer Prize for *Beyond the Horizon.* (Courtesy Shaeffer-O'Neill Collection, Charles E. Shain Library, Connecticut College, New London, Conn.)

German U-Boat 156 shelling coal barges off Nauset, 1918. Painting by Frank Milby. (Courtesy Chatham Historical Society)

game in Provincetown.) Carrying no bombs, the pilot dropped a monkey wrench onto the U-boat; how effective this was is unknown. The U-boat, either satisfied with sinking the barges, or intimidated by the monkey wrench, slipped beneath the surface. A Coast Guard boat picked up survivors. The shells fired at the beach in Orleans were the first foreign attack on American soil since 1815.

Fortunately for other barges, the Cape Cod Canal, proposed by Myles Standish in 1623 and urged by George Washington in 1775, finally opened in 1914. A boost in maritime trade in the 1880s resulted in more wrecks on the outer Cape, and the New York financier August Belmont stepped in to finish the canal. Digging began in 1909; the project took five years to complete. The U.S. government bought it in 1928 and widened it to 480 feet, making it the world's widest sea-level canal. Sparing mariners the outer Cape shoals, it cut 135 miles from the Boston–New York route.

At this time, for the first time since the 1850s, the Cape's population grew. The automobile, rising wages, and paid vacations, all becoming prominent in the years after the Great War, made Cape

The Cape Cod Canal did not prevent maritime disasters, as the steamship *Belfast* crashed into the Sagamore drawbridge, April 19, 1919. (Photograph by Fred C. Small; courtesy Nina Heald Webber Collection, Historic New England)

The Bourne Bridge, newly built over the Cape Cod Canal, in the 1930s. (Courtesy Nina Heald Webber Collection, Historic New England)

In wartime the Cape's beaches, such as Falmouth's Silver Beach, were perfect for practicing amphibious landings, as shown in this June 1941 photo. (Acme Photo; courtesy Historic New England)

Cod a vacation destination. The newly formed Cape Cod Chamber of Commerce vigorously marketed the Cape to tourists. The Great Depression put the brakes on development, but at the end of the 1930s the Cape's first motel opened at Craigville. Thousands of young servicemen training at Camp Edwards and Camp Wellfleet during World War II, or serving on ships stopping in Provincetown, saw firsthand the Cape's unique beauty and came back. Between 1950 and 1970 the Cape's population doubled, and it had doubled again by 1990.

When a new highway from the Sagamore Bridge to Hyannis opened in 1950, and a four-lane highway connected Truro and Provincetown five years later, the artist Hans Hoffman predicted the end of Provincetown's art colony. The highway would bring in floods of visitors. This would be good for the local economy but would price out artists and eventually even fishermen. Provincetown as a resort, he predicted, would lose the unique character that made it attractive in the first place.

The upper Cape had already changed. The writer Scott Corbett settled in East Dennis in 1951 and wrote two books, *We Chose Cape Cod* and *Cape Cod's Way,* about the fishing village they now called home. By the end of the decade the Corbetts had moved to Rhode Island. "Neat new colonies are sprouting everywhere," he wrote, "full of people who are all very nice and all look exactly alike. The simple little harbor I wrote about, with its fishermen in rowboats with 5-horsepower motors, is now full of suburbanites and 35-horsepower monstrosities."

Worries about the Cape's development and loss of character coincided with expansive ideas about the federal government's power. The National Park Service in 1939 considered protecting the entire Massachusetts Bay coastline from Duxbury to Provincetown. Nothing came of it at the time, and development took off after the war. The Massachusetts Department of Commerce in 1955 called the rate of the Cape's development "almost an emergency," and Cape Cod's Chamber of Commerce proposed creating a Regional Planning District to prevent unbridled development. Chambers of commerce usually do not restrict economic development, but the chamber's leaders understood that the Cape's natural environment was its main resource.

The National Park Service made preserving the Cape's outer beaches its top priority. Though privately owned, most of the outer Cape from Monomoy to the Province Lands was still undeveloped in the 1950s. Strong support to preserve the shoreline came from those with a recreational or artistic interest in the Cape, such as State Natural Resources Commissioner Francis Sargent, founder of the Goose Hummock sporting goods shop in Orleans.

Most Cape towns took a shorter view. Development generated tax revenues. Town leaders and property owners were reluctant to restrict their tax base or give away their rights to develop their own property. Congressmen Thomas P. O'Neill of Cambridge and Edward Boland of Springfield were "booed out town hall in Eastham and were hung in effigy in Truro" when they came to propose creating the National Seashore.

Provincetown tried to acquire the 3,000-acre Province Lands, which had belonged to Massachusetts since before Provincetown was incorporated. The town commissioned a master plan, envisioning high-rise buildings and a heliport, an Inland Sea Parkway, a Bayshore Parkway, and a Pilgrim's Crossing Viaduct connecting Provincetown to Plymouth. The stunning plan prompted two Provincetown artists, Josephine Del Deo and Ross Moffett, to form the Emergency Committee for the Preservation of the Province Lands. The Provincetown Town Meeting thwarted the town's ambition, voting 144–61 to turn all the Province Lands over to the Cape Cod National Seashore.

Senators Leverett Saltonstall, a Republican, and John F. Kennedy, a Democrat who spent his summers in Hyannis Port, pushed the measure through the Senate, and Congressman Hastings Keith, representing the Cape, steered it through the House. One Nevada senator, reluctant to support the government's taking private property, supported the proposal when he saw the lands above Eastham's Nauset Bay staked for subdivision.

Congress created the Cape Cod National Seashore, and President John F. Kennedy signed the bill into law on August 7, 1961. The Seashore today includes 27,700 acres of land, and 17,000 acres of water and wetlands. State parks, including Massachusetts' first, the Rowland C. Nickerson Park in Brewster, protect another 30,000 acres. In addition, many towns have conservation areas, and individuals have created private preserves.

Kurt Vonnegut

OCCUPATION: Writer; proprietor of second American Saab dealership, Barnstable, 1950s; English teacher for one year in Sandwich

LIFETIME: 1922–2007

HOMETOWN: Barnstable, 1951–71.

FAMILY: Born in Indianapolis. Married Jane Marie Cox, 1945; three children; adopted three nephews after sister and brother-in-law's deaths, 1958. Moved to New York, 1971, divorced; married Jill Krementz, 1979.

ACCOMPLISHMENTS: Fourteen novels include _Cat's Cradle_ (1963), _Slaughterhouse Five_ (1969), _Breakfast of Champions_ (1973).

Kurt Vonnegut

> _"Few Cape villages have much chance of coming through the present greedy, tasteless boom with their souls intact. H. L. Mencken once said something to the effect that 'Nobody ever went broke overestimating the vulgarity of the American people,' and fortunes now being made out of the vulgarization of the Cape surely bear this out. The soul of Barnstable Village just might survive."_
> —From "Where I Live," in _Welcome to the Monkey House_ (1968)

The land was protected, though communities' characters changed. Hyannis, with the construction of highways and the opening of its airport, and its links by ferry to Nantucket and Martha's Vineyard, became the Cape's main "city," although it is still a village in the town of Barnstable. With its malls and other amenities, it is more urban than the longtime Cape metropolises, Provincetown and Falmouth.

Edward Hopper painted this Eastham farm in 1941; Route 6 running past it would soon change its rural isolation. (Courtesy Swope Art Museum, Terre Haute, Ind.)

The rest of the upper Cape from Sandwich to Yarmouth is within a reasonable commute of Boston; these towns have become suburbs of Boston or retirement havens.

At midcentury, between the sprawl of Hyannis and the streets of Falmouth, lay the still undeveloped woods and ponds of Mashpee, where Solomon Attaquin had first introduced wealthy and powerful whites to the natural resources of the Cape. Developers bought up these tracts in the 1950s and 1960s, and for the first time whites outnumbered Indians in the town. The Mashpees had enjoyed the right to fish in the coastal waters since Richard Bourne had purchased the lands in the 1660s; they now found themselves shut out, and they lost control of the town government. The Mashpees sued in the 1970s, citing laws passed in 1790s and 1834 forbidding private sale of Indian land. They lost the bitter suit, but it awakened the Mashpees to their lost destiny. They began the process of securing federal recognition as a tribe. In a complicated arrangement with the town government, the Mashpees agreed that if they achieved federal recognition, they would not open a casino (as Indians were permitted to do under a 1988 federal law) on Cape Cod. The Bureau

Two Hyannis Port sailors, Edward M. Kennedy (left) and his brother John F. Kennedy prepare to hoist a sail. (Courtesy John F. Kennedy Library and Museum)

Congressman Thomas P. "Tip" O'Neill, Lieutenant Governor Elliot Richardson, and Senator Leverett Saltonstall came to Eastham, May 30, 1966, to dedicate the Cape Cod National Seashore. (Courtesy Massachusetts Historical Society)

John Peters/Slow Turtle

OCCUPATION: Medicine man, Mashpee Wampanoag; first executive director, Massachusetts Commissioner for Indian Affairs (1974–97)

LIFETIME: 1930–97

HOMETOWN: Mashpee

FAMILY: Son of a Mashpee selectman. Married three times; five daughters and seven sons.

ACCOMPLISHMENTS: Secured state passage of law requiring repatriation of Indian remains; helped secure passage of American Indian Religious Freedom Act and Indian Child Welfare Act (1978).

John Peters

"What every American Indian must learn to do is keep both feet on shore, remain an Indian, but also understand the need to occasionally sail into the white man's territory to survive."

of Indian Affairs in 2007 recognized the Mashpee Wampanoags as a tribe.

Artists were drawn to Provincetown by the light; writers were drawn by the artists. Wives and widows of fishermen rented them rooms. Valuing their own privacy, Provincetown's people did not meddle in their guests' affairs, and by the 1950s Provincetown was one of the few places in the country where gay men and women could vacation without fear of arrest. In the 1970s and 1980s, as gays broke down the constraints that had forced them into the closet, Provincetown remained an inviting and welcoming place. By the 1990s the gay population came to dominate the town. As gays and lesbians win acceptance in other parts of the country, and as Provincetown's cost of living escalates, will the town continue to be a special destination for gay men and women, or will they, like the artists and writers, the Pilgrims and fishermen before them, find other havens?

When Gosnold's men anchored in Provincetown Harbor, there seemed to be no end of fish. The native people harvested crabs, clams, oysters, and herring without number. But by the twentieth century the fish were running out, and the small commercial fishermen were pushed out by factory ships and bottom-stripping trawlers; pollution of the water also contributed to the decline in numbers of fish. In the 1980s the U.S. government limited the amount of fish that could be caught offshore. Intended to help the fish rebound, in the short run the limitations put small fishermen on the same path as the small farmer and the windmill operator.

Two Provincetown fishermen, Al and Justin Avellar, noticed in the 1960s that they were catching fewer fish but seeing more whales. They started to take visitors out on their fishing boat to see the mammals that had made nineteenth-century Cape Codders rich. In 1975 they converted their fishing boat into a passenger-carrying whale-watch boat, creating a new industry—whale watching—which brings thousands of people to the tip of Cape Cod. From April to October visitors can voyage out to Stellwagen Bank, formerly a rich fishing area, to watch whales feed in a newly designated federal marine sanctuary.

The subjects of Chaim Gross's statue, *Tourists*, in front of Provincetown's library, are forever intrigued and baffled by the scene on Commercial Street, as seen in the painting by Mary Spencer Nay. (Collection of the Town of Provincetown, courtesy Provincetown Art Commission)

Dr. Charles "Stormy" Mayo, descended from Cape Cod whalers, created the Center for Coastal Studies in Provincetown to study marine life, particularly whales. A collaboration between the scientists from the Center for Coastal Studies and the operators of whale-watch cruises has increased our understanding of the lives of whales and the threats to their survival. Since 1984 the center has rescued whales entangled in fishing gear and helped these mammals recover from the brink of extinction.

Francis "Flyer" Santos

OCCUPATION: Boatbuilder; founder of Flyer's Boat Yard

HOMETOWN: Provincetown

LIFETIME: 1914–

FAMILY: Grandson of a whaler; married Irene Maille, 1940; six children.

Accomplishments: Served on Provincetown Board of Selectmen, Provincetown School Committee, most local committees; founded West End Racing Club (1950) to teach sailing and swimming; built scale-model replica of schooner *Rose Dorothea* in Provincetown Library.

Francis Santos

Watching West End Racing Club members roughhousing on the club float: *"Those kids learn more on that float—or taking a boat across the harbor—than they do from any schoolteacher or in any classroom. They come from all over the world and learn to get along."*

Glaciers and ocean currents shaped Cape Cod; men and women have shaped its history. But in the sand and water we leave no mark. Fishermen and farmers, Native people and Pilgrims, Yankees and Portuguese, gays and retirees, tourists and revivalists, hunters and artists have all passed over the sands of the Cape, trying to impress their mark on the shifting spit of land. Our mark will be as indelible as that made by those who have gone before. Those who come thinking they have discovered it, believing they can own it, are mocked by the Atlantic currents and northeast winds, by the laughing gulls and diving cormorants.

The Cape's economy continues to follow the whales. (Courtesy of the artist, Robert Clibbon)

Provincetown's Center for Coastal Studies rescues a right whale entangled in fishing gear. (Courtesy Provincetown Center for Coastal Studies)

chronology

c. 1000   Bjarni Herjólfsson, a Viking, sails southwest from Iceland, perhaps sees but does not set foot on Cape Cod.

c. 1004   Another Viking, Thorwald, repairs his ship in a place he calls Keelness, now Provincetown.

1600s

1602   May: Bartholomew Gosnold visits the Cape, names it Cape Cod, also names Elizabeth Islands for Queen Elizabeth (or his wife) and Martha's Vineyard for his daughter.

1606   Samuel de Champlain and a French expedition visit Monomoy (Chatham). Plague strikes the Native population.

1614   John Smith draws a map of an area he names New England, calls Cape Cod "Cape James." Captain Hunt kidnaps Tisquantum and fourteen Nausets. Adrian Block visits area, calls the Cape "Staaten Hook."

1619   Thomas Dermer takes Tisquantum to Sauquatuckett, the northwestern part of Harwich.

1620   Pilgrims find refuge in Provincetown Harbor, sign the Mayflower Compact. Peregrine White is born on the *Mayflower* in Provincetown Harbor.

1622   Tisquantum, or Squanto, dies on a trading mission with Bradford to Monomoyick Bay (now Chatham).

1623   Threat of attacks from Pilgrims drives Sachems Iyanough of Cummaquid, Canacum of Manomet, and Aspinet of Nauset into the swamps, where they die of smallpox, which kills many other Indians and prevents planting.

1626   December: Wreck of the *Sparrowhawk*, the Pilgrim's shallop, in Potonumequot harbor; wreck gives name to Old Ship Beach, Orleans.

Frank Milby, a Provincetown artist, depicts whalers at work

1627   Pilgrims open a trading post at Aptucxet, on Manomet River, to trade with Wamponoags, Narragansetts, and the Dutch.

1637   Sixty families are given permission to settle at Shawme (Sandwich). Stephen Bachiler and his band briefly stay in a part of Mattacheese that will later be Barnstable.

1639   Sandwich is incorporated, the fourth town in Plymouth Colony. Anthony Thacher and two others are given grants to settle in a part of Mattacheese that is now Yarmouth. Rev. John Lothrop and twenty-five families settle in Barnstable.

1646   Nauset settlement (now Eastham) is incorporated.

1649   John Crocker opens the first tavern in Barnstable.

1651   Cape Cod towns agree to send to colonial government one barrel of oil from every whale caught.

1652   David and Hannah Linnel, married just three months, are publicly whipped in Barnstable for "fornication . . . before marriage."

1654   Samson, sachem of the Nausets, sells Province Lands to Plymouth Colony. John Smith is paid to carry letters from Plymouth to Nauset.

1660   Richard Bourne secures a deed from Quatchatisset to establish Mashpee as an Indian settlement.

1663 Edward Sturgis of Yarmouth loses his liquor license for failing to notify authorities how much liquor he imported into town.

1665 Pompmo and Simon sell land at Weguasset, or Round Cove, now Harwich, to Josiah Cook.

1666 Sachem Yanno sells South Barnstable to Nicholas Davis.

1670 Richard Bourne organizes an Indian church at Mashpee.

1680 John Gorham of Barnstable goes whaling in the ship *Lopez.*

1681 First school is established in Barnstable, supported by taxes on Provincetown fisheries.

1682 Indians at Potanumaquut (South Orleans) establish their own court and magistracy with General Court's permission.

1683 Colonists learn to make cranberry juice.

1684 An Indian church is built at Mashpee.

1685 First Barnstable County Court House is built, as Plymouth Colony establishes Barnstable County.

1686 Falmouth is incorporated.

1689 Thomas Macy builds first fulling (cleansing wool or fabric) mill in Barnstable, Marston's Mills.

1690 Nantucket residents ask Ichabod Paddock of Yarmouth to teach them fine points of whaling.

1697 Massachusetts government studies possibility of digging a canal between Cape Cod and Buzzards Bay.

1699 First Congregational Church, Falmouth, is gathered.

1700s

1705 John Stacey is given permission to dam Goodspeed River, Cotuit, to build a mill.

1709 The town of Truro is incorporated (had been settled as Dangerfield about 1705).

1712 The town of Chatham is incorporated.

1714 Massachusetts sets aside Province Lands, near Provincetown, to restrict tree cutting.

1717 A storm opens a channel from Rock Harbor to Nauset.

1718 Falmouth offers Hannah Sargent a job of keeping a school, for £12 plus board each year, to alternate through four quarters of town every year; she declines.

1725 Rev. Josiah Dennis becomes pastor in Yarmouth's East Parish (later named the town of Dennis).

1727 Provincetown is incorporated.

1734 Eastham, Harwich, Chatham, Provincetown, and Truro petition unsuccessfully to be separated from Barnstable County.

1747 Yarmouth gives three proprietors permission to build a windmill in East Parish (now Dennis).

1750 The Bray family opens a shipyard in Yarmouth.

1763 Billingsgate (Wellfleet) is set off from Eastham.

1764 Eastham and Harwich establish a boundary.

1765 Cape Cod population is approximately 12,000. Smallpox kills thirty-seven in Chatham.

1770 Wellfleet oysters die off.

1771 Barnstable builds the first schoolhouse on Cape Cod.

1772 General Court cedes Potanumaquut, the northeastern part of Harwich—now South Orleans—to Eastham.

1773 Sandwich Town Meeting instructs its delegates to General Court to end the slave trade and gradually emancipate Massachusetts slaves. Virus kills Falmouth oysters.

1774   September 6: 1,500 Patriots prevent the Court of Common Pleas from sitting, protesting a new rule allowing the sheriff to appoint jurors and having the court sit at the king's pleasure. October: Falmouth Town Meeting appoints a Committee of Correspondence and votes that every man sixteen to sixty be equipped with ammunition and arms.

1775   October 11: The Barnstable hangman publicly burns symbols of royal authority outside the Barnstable courthouse. The Provincial Congress establishes a mail route from Cambridge to Falmouth.

1776   The widow Nabby Freeman, a Barnstable Tory, is tarred and feathered and paraded around Barnstable on a rail. George Washington sends the engineer Thomas Machin to study a possible canal between Buzzards Bay and Cape Cod Bay; Machin recommends a 7½-mile-long, 14-foot-deep canal with locks on either end. John Sears builds the first saltworks at Sesuit Harbor, East Dennis. Cape Cod population is approximately 14,000.

1777   A smallpox epidemic hits the Cape; many Native Americans die.

1778   April 3: The British fleet attempts to burn Falmouth, but is repulsed by militia. November 3: The *Somerset* wrecks on outer bars off Provincetown.

1787   Captain John Kendrick sails on the *Columbia* from Boston for Pacific Northwest.

1790   Cape Cod population is 17,000.

1792   First mail service between Barnstable and Boston is established.

1793   East Parish of Yarmouth is incorporated as the town of Dennis; the first Methodist minister arrives in Provincetown, "windbound in Provincetown Harbor."

1794   First Methodist Church is built in Truro, the second in New England; Thacher windmill is built in Yarmouth.

1795   Rev. Joseph Snelling, a Methodist, arrives in Truro. A Methodist society is formed in Provincetown, and a mob burns wood intended to build the meetinghouse. Falmouth prohibits hogs from running wild

Chatham Light.

in town. The first Post Office opens in Yarmouth. Scorton windmill is built at Sandy Neck; it is later moved to West Dennis and later still to South Yarmouth. King Hiram's Lodge, Ancient Free and Accepted Masons, is organized in Provincetown.

1797   South Parish of Eastham becomes the town of Orleans. June 12: Highland Light, Cape Cod's first lighthouse, is lit. A smallpox epidemic hits the Cape, and Falmouth establishes a smallpox hospital on Nobska. A windmill is built in Chatham. Peter Baker builds a windmill in South Dennis. A weekly mail route between Yarmouth and Truro is initiated.

1800s

1800   Cape Cod population is 19,293.

1801   Fraternal Lodge (Masons) is formed in Barnstable. A smallpox outbreak occurs in Provincetown.

1802   The First Masonic Hall is built in Barnstable.

1803   North Parish of Harwich becomes the town of Brewster. Sandwich Academy is founded.

1804   Jeremiah's Gutter (a narrow shortcut for small vessels), dug in 1717, is widened and improved between Rock Harbor and Nauset inlet.

1805   The Town of Harwich builds the first bridge over the Herring River.

1808   Chatham Lights are established.

1810   Cape Cod population is 21,372.

1812   Congressman Isaiah L. Green of Barnstable is defeated for reelection after voting for the War of 1812.

Highland Light.

1814   The British bombard Falmouth and attack Orleans.

1815   September: A hurricane joins Manomet River with Scusset Creek, takes the roof off Jeremiah Walker's windmill at Harwich, and destroys Falmouth's town wharf. A lighthouse is built at Point Gammon, Yarmouth.

1816   An epidemic sweeps the outer Cape. Captain Henry Hall discovers that cranberry bogs covered in sand produce more berries. Race Point Lighthouse is built.

1817   The second Temperance Society in the U.S. is formed in Yarmouth. Eastham and Orleans Canal Proprietors is incorporated, to open the canal at Jeremiah's Gutter.

1818   November: John Atwood constructs the first building on Long Point, in Provincetown.

1819   The first religious revival meeting is held in South Wellfleet.

1820   The *Truth,* offering regular packet service between Boston and Provincetown, begins sailing. Lower Cape towns reject semiweekly mail service as too expensive. Cape Cod population is 24,431.

1821   Falmouth Bank, the first bank on the Cape, is founded.

1822   Emmanuel Caton is the first Portuguese person to settle in Provincetown.

1823   Monomoy Light is established. The Cape's first newspaper, the *Falmouth Nautical Intelligencer,* is printed; it does not last.

1824   A cotton factory is opened in Harwich, on Red River; the following year it is moved to Herring River.

Map of Cape Cod in Sandwich glass.

1825   Deming Jarves opens the Sandwich glassworks, Boston & Sandwich Glass Company. The publisher of the *Nautical Intelligencer* starts the *Barnstable Gazette,* published until 1827. The Commonwealth begins planting Dutch beach grass in the dunes of Provincetown to control erosion.

1826   Keith Car and Manufacturing Company opens in Sandwich, builds stagecoaches, wagons, and railroad cars. The *Barnstable Journal* begins publication. Long Point Lighthouse, Provincetown, is built. A religious revival meeting is held in Truro.

1827   Fire destroys the Barnstable Court House. Construction begins on the Hyannis breakwater (finished 1837).

1828   Nobska Point Lighthouse is built. Religious revival meetings begin in Eastham. A Temperance Society is formed in Barnstable. A Baptist church is established in Orleans.

1829   St. Peter's Catholic Church, the first Catholic church on the Cape, is built in Sandwich. The Universalist Society is organized in Barnstable.

1830   The *Barnstable Patriot* begins publication. Cape Cod population is 28,525.

1832   The *Barnstable Journal* becomes the *Cape Cod Journal.*

1833   Residents of Mashpee protest whites from neighboring towns cutting wood on their land. Universalist Societies are organized in Provincetown and Orleans.

1834   Mashpee achieves self-government as an Indian town.

1835   The first wharf is built in Provincetown.

1838   Nauset Light (Three Sisters) shines for first time. The *Cape Cod Journal* moves to Yarmouth, becomes the *Yarmouth Register,* and continues to 1890. Daily mail service as far as Yarmouth is established. Provincetown installs a wooden sidewalk on Front Street (now Commercial Street). Cape Cod population is 31,109.

1839   A gale destroys twenty Provincetown salt mills. The last wolf is shot in Sandwich. During Barnstable's bicentennial, women are invited to join men at a celebratory banquet.

1840   Cape Cod population is 32,199.

1841   A gale on October 3 kills fifty-seven men from Truro, twenty-eight from Dennis.

1842   The legislature calls for a division of Mashpee lands, along with restrictions on sales to non-Mashpees.

1843   The Agricultural Society is formed and begins holding the annual Barnstable County Fair.

1844   Sidney Brooks founds Brooks Seminary, Harwich. The *Sandwich Observer* begins publication. The last whaling voyage sails from Barnstable.

1847   The first wharf is erected in Harwich, at Marsh Bank. A Universalist church is built in Provincetown. Daily mail service begins from Yarmouth to Orleans, and from Orleans to Provincetown.

1848   May 26: The first train reaches Sandwich, connecting the Cape with Plymouth and Boston. The last schooner is built in Harwich.

1849   Henry David Thoreau makes his first visit to Cape Cod. Pamet Harbor lighthouse is built.

1850   The Shiverick family of Dennis begins building clipper ships. Thoreau visits Cape Cod for the second time. A Roman Catholic society is organized in Barnstable. Cape Cod population is 33,979.

1851   The first Catholic Mass is celebrated in Provincetown. Seamen's Savings Bank is incorporated at Union Wharf, Provincetown. South Truro Meeting House opens. The *Sandwich Observer* moves to North Bridgewater (now Brockton).

1852   The last whaler sails from Truro.

1853   A marker is placed in front of Provincetown Town Hall commemorating the arrival of the Pilgrims.

1854   The railroad reaches Barnstable, Yarmouth, and Hyannis, with connections to Nantucket steamers. An unsuccessful attempt is made to dredge Pamet Harbor. Provincetown and Truro build a bridge across East Harbor; a storm destroys it following year; it is rebuilt in 1856.

1855   Thoreau visits Cape Cod for the third time. Pamet Light is discontinued. The *Provincetown Banner* begins publication (lasts until 1862).

1857   Thoreau makes final visit to Cape Cod. *Cape Cod News* is published at Provincetown. Cape Cod population is 35,877.

1859   Last whaling voyage sails from Falmouth; the last Falmouth whaler is sold in 1864.

1860   Governor Nathaniel Banks revives the prospect of a canal. A Methodist church is built in Provincetown (now Provincetown Public Library). Cape Cod population is 35,990.

1862   The legislature sets a boundary in the bay between Chatham and Harwich. Pacific Guano Company is founded in Woods Hole. The *Cape Cod Republican* is established at Harwich. The last whaler sails from Sandwich.

The Methodist Church, now the Provincetown Library, rises over the East End in Robert Clibbon's print. (Courtesy Robert Clibbon)

1863   Captain William Sturgis gives his house (built in 1644) to the trustees of the Barnstable Public Library, along with $15,000. Captains Levi Howes and Allison Howes of Dennis race their ships, *Belle of the West* and *Starlight,* from Calcutta to Boston. A religious revival meeting is held in Yarmouth.

1865   The railroad reaches Orleans. The *Sparrowhawk* is exhumed and taken to Boston Common, then Providence, Rhode Island (now in Pilgrim Hall Museum, Plymouth). Cape Cod population is 34,489.

1869   Indians in Massachusetts become citizens, and the legislature calls for Mashpee lands to be divided and sold. The *Provincetown Advocate* begins publication.

1870   The railroad reaches Wellfleet. The legislature incorporates Mashpee as a town. The *Provincetown News* begins and ends publication. Cape Cod population is 32,500.

1871   The *Chatham Monitor* begins publication, printed by the *Barnstable Patriot.* Hyannis Land Company is formed to begin real estate development of Hyannis Port.

1872   The U.S. Life-Saving Service established; a life-saving station is built at Monomoy. The railroad line is extended to Woods Hole, and Nantucket steamers call there rather than Hyannis. Ministers from Rhode Island hold a summer retreat in what becomes Craigville. The *Harwich Independent*, printed by the *Barnstable Patriot*, begins publication. There is a smallpox outbreak in Provincetown.

1873   The railroad reaches Provincetown. Wood End Light is built in Provincetown.

1874   President Ulysses S. Grant visits Cape Cod, traveling by train from Hyannis to Provincetown. Provincetown Harbor is completely iced in. St. Peter the Apostle Church is built in Provincetown.

1877   Fire destroys Provincetown Town Hall. A causeway is built over East Harbor, connecting Provincetown to Truro.

1878   The *Cape Cod Item* is established at Yarmouth Port.

1879   August 18: Hurricane hits. A cable connects Eastham with Europe by way of the French island of St. Pierre-Miquelon, off Newfoundland.

1880   The *Barnstable Patriot* publishes the *Cape Cod Bee*, at Wellfleet. Cape Cod population is 32,000.

1881   The publisher of the *Cape Cod Item* issues the *Mayflower*, a story and feature journal (until 1889).

1882   Telephone service is established in parts of Cape Cod.

1883   The Marine Biological Station (later merged into the Marine Biological Laboratory) is established at Woods Hole.

1884   The Town of Bourne separates from Sandwich. The *Sandwich Observer* begins publication, by the *Barnstable Patriot*.

1885   The Harwich Exchange Building is dedicated; at 104 feet high, it is the tallest commercial building ever built on Cape Cod. Cape Cod Baseball League is founded. Lorenzo Dow Baker converts the abandoned Mercantile Wharf in Wellfleet into the Chequesset Inn.

1886   The *Falmouth Local* begins publication. The *Barnstable County Journal*, at the time the only Democratic paper on the Cape, begins publication (ceases in 1890).

The crumbling ruins of the Sandwich glassworks. (Historic New England)

1887   The railroad is extended from Harwich to Chatham. The *Cape Cod News* begins publication in South Yarmouth (absorbed by the *Item* in 1888).

1888   The Sandwich glassworks shuts down in a labor dispute. The last Cape Cod salt mill, on Bass River, ceases operation. Cape Cod Cranberry Growers Association is formed. The Marine Biological Laboratory opens in Woods Hole.

1889   The *Sparrowhawk* is taken to Pilgrim Hall, Plymouth. Vacation bungalows are built at Ballston Beach, Truro.

1890   Former President Grover Cleveland purchases Gray Gables, a home on Monument River, in Bourne. District courts are established in Barnstable and Provincetown. Cape Cod population is 29,000.

1891   The French Cable Station moves from Eastham to Orleans.

1892   Fire destroys much of the Hyannis business district. The *Chatham Gazette* begins publication.

Lifesaving drill at Chatham Life-Saving Station. (Chatham Historical Society)

1893   A gardener, Michael Walsh, raises first "rambler rose" in Woods Hole.

1895   John Simpkins of Yarmouth is elected to the U.S. House of Representatives (serves until 1898).

1896   A storm pushes the ocean through to Pamet River, Truro.

1897   Hyannis Normal School opens, one of four state teacher colleges. The Nickerson family holds a reunion—a "general meeting"—in Chatham. Jackson Williams begins building Captain Jack's Wharf, Provincetown.

1898   Highland Links in Truro is established. The Portland Gale occurs on November 27. Old Harbor Life-Saving Station is built in Chatham. Cable connects Orleans with Brest, France.

1899   Charles W. Hawthorne establishes an art school in Provincetown.

1900s

1900   Cape Cod population is 27,826.

1901   Corpus Christi Roman Catholic Church replaces St. Peter's in Sandwich, which was damaged in the Portland Gale.

1902   Lorenzo Dow Baker subsidizes the first steam-powered oyster boat in Wellfleet.

1904   Marconi establishes a wireless station in Wellfleet. Joseph C. Lincoln publishes his first novel, *Cap'n Eri*. A December 2–3 fire destroys the Hyannis business district.

1907   The Provincetown schooner *Rose Dorothea* wins the Fisherman's Race at Boston's Old Home Week, defeating Gloucester boats and winning the Lipton Cup. President Theodore Roosevelt lays the cornerstone for the Pilgrim Monument in Provincetown.

1909   Work begins on the Cape Cod Canal.

Marconi's radio towers in Wellfleet.

1910   Cranberry Experiment Station opens at Wareham. President William Howard Taft presides at the dedication of the Pilgrim Monument. Cape Cod population is 27,542.

1911   The original Bourne Bridge, a drawbridge, opens. Provincetown's West End breakwater is built.

1913   The original Sagamore Bridge, also a drawbridge, and a railroad bridge open. Barnstable Customs District merges with Boston district.

1914   The Cape Cod Canal opens. The Provincetown Art Association is formed. Chatham Bars Inn opens.

1915   Provincetown Players is established. More than sixty artists display works in a Provincetown Town Hall show sponsored by Provincetown Art Association. Construction begins on Provincetown Inn. John Walsh (born in Falmouth) is elected to Congress from the district that includes the Cape (serves until 1921).

Two men in their bathing suits, 1911, Orleans. (Orleans Historical Society)

1916   Eugene O'Neill's *Bound East for Cardiff* is performed by Provincetown Players. Charles Henry Davis of South Yarmouth installs the first traffic rotary in the country.

1917   Eugene O'Neill's *Ile*, based on the voyage of John and Viola Cook, is premiered by Provincetown Players in Greenwich Village. The Marconi wireless station ceases operations.

1918   German U-boat 156 destroys the tugboat *Perth Amboy* as it shells barges off Nauset Inlet.

1920   Cape Cod Hospital opens in Hyannis in response to flu epidemic of 1918–19. Provincetown unveils a bas relief on the 300th anniversary of the Pilgrims' landing. O'Neill wins a Pulitzer Prize for *Beyond the Horizon*. Cape Cod population is 26,670.

Postcard view of the Cape Cod Canal

1921   Cape Cod Chamber of Commerce founded. Provincetown Art Association moves into permanent home at 460 Commercial Street. Charles Gifford of Cotuit is elected to U.S. Congress (serves until 1947). Shawme State Forest is set aside in Bourne and Sandwich.

1925   The schooner *John R. Manta* of Provincetown returns from the last
       New England whaling voyage.
1926   Dennis buys its first public beach in Dennis Port. Electricity comes
       to Eastham.
1927   The Cape Playhouse opens in Dennis. Submarine S-4 is lost off
       Provincetown with forty men. Walter Smith, Provincetown's full-
       time town crier, retires. Donald Ross designs a golf course at
       Oyster Harbors Club in Osterville. Harry Aldrich moves a tower
       from Fitchburg Railroad Depot, Boston, to Truro, as a memorial to
       Jenny Lind, the Swedish soprano who sang from it in the 1850s.

Charles Demuth's abstract rendering of Provincetown's Methodist church, 1919. (Courtesy McNay Art Museum, San Antonio)

1928   The financier Joseph P. Kennedy purchases a vacation home in
       Hyannis Port. Henry Beston publishes *The Outermost House*, about a
       year spent in an Eastham beach shack; J. C. Penney Jr. establishes a
       gliding school at Corn Hill, Truro (the school later moves to
       Wellfleet).
1929   The first organized Wampanoag powwow is held in Mashpee.
1930   Dr. Frederick Hammett establishes the Marine Experimental
       Station (part of the Lankenau Hospital Research Institute in North
       Truro), using marine life to study the biological basis of cancer. Dr.
       Oliver Austin creates Austin Ornithological Research Station in
       South Wellfleet. Keith Car Company closes. Ocean Spray
       Cranberry, Inc., a growers' cooperative, is founded. Cape Cod pop-
       ulation is 32,305.
1932   Hyannis Normal School becomes a state teachers' college.
1933   Cape Cod Jewish Women's Club is founded; the following year
       these women spark creation of Cape Cod's first synagogue, in
       Hyannis.
1934   Hans Hofmann opens an art school in Provincetown.

Provincetown's town crier.

1935   The new Sagamore and Bourne bridges open. The State estab-
       lishes a National Guard training camp in Bourne, Sandwich, and
       Falmouth (later Camp Edwards).
1936   The *Cape Cod Standard Times,* distributed by the *New Bedford
       Standard-Times,* begins publication in Hyannis.
1937   Rowland C. Nickerson State Park, the first park owned by
       Commonwealth of Massachusetts, opens in Brewster. A storm
       causes a breach in the dunes at Pamet River, Truro. Otis Air Field is
       established in Sandwich, Mashpee, and Falmouth.

Automap postcard from the late 1930s.

1938   Rail service is suspended east of Yarmouth. A severe hurricane
       strikes in September.
1939   Sunny Sands Motel, the first Cape motel, opens at
       Craigville Beach. The National Park Service investigates
       the possibility of preserving the shoreline from Duxbury
       to Provincetown.
1940   Cape Cod population is 37,295.
1942   Massachusetts Nautical School (founded 1891) moves
       from Boston to Hyannis and becomes Massachusetts
       Maritime Academy.
1943   German prisoners of war are incarcerated at Camp
       Edwards.

Cape Codders vote in Alice Stallknecht's mural Every Man to His Trade, *1945. (Chatham Historical Society)*

1944   A hurricane hits Cape Cod. Monomoy Island is desig-
       nated as a wildlife preserve.
1946   Willis Gould, his son Bill, and Francis "Sarge" Sargent open
       Goose Hummock sporting goods shop in Orleans.

1948	Twenty-nine Latvian refugees arrive in Provincetown from England after forty-three days at sea.
1949	Massachusetts Maritime Academy moves to Buzzards Bay.
1950	The two-lane Mid-Cape Highway (now Route 6) opens from Sagamore Bridge to Exit 6, West Barnstable. The Cape Cod Music Circus (now Cape Cod Melody Tent) opens in Hyannis. Cape population is 46,805.

A sportsman in Eastham. (Orleans Historical Society)

1952	Coast Guard 36500 rescues thirty-three men off the tanker *Pendleton*, battered in a storm.
1954	Hurricanes Carol (August 31) and Edna (September 11) batter Cape Cod.
1955	The Commonwealth purchases 733 acres at High Head in Truro. Fire destroys the Indian-run Hotel Attaquin in Mashpee.
1956	The four-lane Route 6 opens between Provincetown and North Truro.
1957	Patti Page records "Old Cape Cod," lyrics by Claire Rothrock and Milt Yakus, music by Allan Jeffrey.
1958	Massachusetts Audubon Society purchases Austin Ornithological Research Station and creates Wellfleet Bay Wildlife Sanctuary. Walter Chrysler establishes Chrysler Art Museum in Provincetown's former Methodist church.

Tourists arrive in Provincetown.

1959	June 30: Year-round regular passenger train service to Cape Cod ends. November: Trans-Atlantic cable stops operations via Orleans. The two-lane Mid-Cape Highway extends to Orleans Rotary.
1960	Cape Cod Community College is founded in West Barnstable. John F. Kennedy of Hyannis Port is elected president of the United States; he delivers his victory speech at Hyannis National Guard Armory. Cape population is 70,286.
1961	Cape Cod National Seashore is established.
1962	Cape Cod Chamber of Commerce begins marketing Cape Cod as a retirement community. New Seabury, a planned resort community, opens on Mashpee's shore. Edward M. Kennedy of Hyannis Port is elected to the U.S. Senate; serves until 2009.
1963	The state completes Route 3 from Boston to the Sagamore Bridge.
1964	The Harwich Exchange Building is demolished.
1965	Salt Pond Visitor Center opens at Cape Cod National Seashore in Eastham.
1968	Fine Arts Work Center is established in Provincetown.
1969	Heritage Plantation opens in Sandwich.
1970	The Coast Guard opens Air Station Cape Cod at Otis Air Force Base, the only Coast Guard rescue station in the Northeast. Cape Cod Mall opens in Hyannis. Restoration is completed on Mashpee's Old Indian Meeting House. Cape Cod population is 96,656.

Cottages on Nauset Beach. (Orleans Historical Society)

1971	The *Cape Cod Standard-Times* becomes an independent paper. Chrysler Art Museum leaves Provincetown for Norfolk, Virginia.
1972	A red tide outbreak destroys shellfish beds. Truro Center for the Arts at Castle Hill begins workshops in converted stables.
1975	Captain Al Avellar of Provincetown begins the first whale-watch cruises. The *Cape Cod Standard-Times* becomes the *Cape Cod Times*.
1976	Provincetown Center for Coastal Studies is established to study and protect whales.
1977	Mashpee Wampanoags lose their lawsuit against New Seabury development.
1978	A February blizzard causes extensive coastal damage, destroying Henry Beston's Outermost House. The first Falmouth Road Race is held.

1979 The Cape Cod Rail Trail, a bike route on former railroad beds, opens.

1980 Cape Cod population is 147,925.

1984 Provincetown Center for Coastal Studies performs the first successful rescue of an entangled whale. Barry Clifford finds the wreck of the *Whydah* (lost in 1717) off Wellfleet. A judge dismisses a case against four Mashpee Indians charged with taking shellfish without a permit.

Marjorie Halper Windust painted Provincetown's East End Cold Storage in 1941. (Courtesy Provincetown Art Commission)

1985 The Northeast Multispecies Fishery Management Plan is implemented to reduce overfishing. Wellfleet Harbor Actors Theater has its first performances.

1990 The Cape Cod Commission is formed to regulate development. Cape Cod population is 186,605.

1991 Hurricane Bob strikes in August; the "No-Name" storm in October causes extensive damage to the coast, including a breach in the dunes at Pamet River.

1992 Stellwagen Bank National Marine Sanctuary is created.

1994 The New England Fishery Management Council further restricts commercial fishermen to protect depleted fish species.

1995 The *Provincetown Banner* begins publication.

1996 Highland Light in Truro is moved back 570 feet from an eroding cliff.

1997 The Environmental Protection Agency orders a stop to military testing at Otis Air Force Base and Camp Edwards in response to pollution of groundwater.

1998 The U.S. Air Force compensates Mashpee and Falmouth cranberry growers for contamination from Otis munitions testing.

2000s

2000 The *Provincetown Banner* buys the *Advocate*, which ceases publication. Cape Cod population is 222,230.

2001 Two F-15s from Otis are first responders to terrorist attacks on New York.

2003 An oil barge hits rocks, leaks 98,000 gallons of crude oil into Buzzards Bay. Provincetown opens a sewer system.

2005 St. Peter the Apostle Church burns in Provincetown. A red tide outbreak destroys shellfish beds. The Rail Trail bike route is extended into Chatham.

2006 Otis Air Force Base becomes Coast Guard Station, Cape Cod.

2007 The federal government recognizes the Mashpee Wampanoags as a tribe. Wellfleet Harbor Actors Theater opens a new year-round theater.

2008 A new St. Peter the Apostle Church is built in Provincetown. A new Our Lady of Lourdes Church opens in Wellfleet.

further reading

THREE INDISPENSABLE BOOKS on Cape Cod's history are Henry David Thoreau's *Cape Cod,* originally published in 1865; Josef Berger's (writing under the pseudonym Jeremiah Digges) *Cape Cod Pilot,* first published in 1937; and William Martin's historical novel *Cape Cod* (1991).

In the 1980s the Massachusetts Historical Commission completed reconnaissance surveys of each of the Cape towns, as well as a general survey of the entire Cape. The MHC Reconnaissance Survey Town Reports (1984–85) are great sources for the history of each town.

Jack Sheedy and Jim Coogan have collected many of their *Barnstable Patriot* historical vignettes in two fine books, *Cape Cod Companion* (1999) and *Cape Cod Voyage* (2001). It is hoped there will be many more in the series. In Provincetown, Laurel Gaudazno, curator of the Pilgrim Monument and Provincetown Museum, has written terrific pieces for both the *Advocate* and the *Banner,* which should be collected in a book. The historical vignettes of Truro's Tom Kane were collected under the title *My Pamet* (1989). Marise Fawsett's *Cape Cod Annals* (1990) and Marion Rawson Vuilleumier's *Sketches of Old Cape Cod* (1972) have great lore. Eugene Green, William Sachse, and Brian McCauley, *The Names of Cape Cod: How Cape Cod Places Got Their Names and What They Mean* (2007), is terrific on the complicated issues of names and pronunciations.

Practically every Cape town had a nineteenth-century history written. Start with Frederick Freeman's *History of Cape Cod* (1858), condensed somewhat in Simeon L. Deyo's *History of Barnstable County, Massachusetts* (1890), and then pick the local histories. David Kew has digitized much of the local history and posted it on his Web site, http://capecodhistory.us.

Town by town, Falmouth to Provincetown: Charles W. Jenkins, *Three Lectures on the History of Falmouth* (1889), and Dorothy Godfrey Wayman, writing under the pseudonym Theodate Geoffrey, *Suckanesset: Wherein May Be Read a History of Falmouth* (1930); Ambrose Pratt, *Two Hundred and Fiftieth Anniversary Celebration of Sandwich and Bourne* (1890), and Betsey Keene, *History of Bourne from 1622 to 1937* (1938); Donald G. Trayser, *Barnstable: Three Centuries of a Cape Cod Town* (1939), written for the town's tricentennial, and the book the town put together for the nation's bicentennial, *The Seven Villages of Barnstable* (1976); Charles Francis Swift, *History of Old Yarmouth* (1884), includes both Yarmouth and Dennis; Josiah Paine, *History of Harwich, 1620–1800* (1937); William C. Smith, *History of Chatham, Massachusetts* (1909); Enoch Pratt, *A Comprehensive History, Ecclesiastical and Civil, of Eastham, Wellfleet, and Orleans* (1844); Durand Echeverria, *A History of Billingsgate* (1993), on Wellfleet's colonial days, is a rewarding book by a professional historian who retired to Wellfleet; Shebnah Rich, *Truro—Cape Cod; or, Land Marks and Sea Marks* (1883); Edmund J. Carpenter, *Provincetown: The Tip of the Cape* (1900) and *The Pilgrims and Their Monument* (1911), Mellen C. M. Hatch, *The Log of Provincetown and Truro on Cape Cod* (1939), and Mary Heaton Vorse, *Time and the Town: A Provincetown Chronicle* (1942).

Mashpee is unique; both a town and a people, the best introductions are Jack Campisi, *The Mashpee Indians: Tribe on Trial* (1991), and Earl Mills Sr. and Alicja Mann, *Son of Mashpee: Reflections of Chief Flying Eagle, a Wampanoag* (2006). Daniel Mandell's *Behind the Frontier: Indians in Eighteenth-century Massachusetts* (1996) and *Tribe, Race, History: Native Americans in Southern New England, 1780–1880* (2008) give an excellent context to the story of Mashpee.

Provincetown is also unique. Some of its facets can be found in the following books. The National Park Service singled out the artist Ross Moffett for his keen sense of history, which is borne out in his *Art in Narrow Streets: The First Thirty-three Years of the Provincetown Art Association* (1989). Leona Rust Egan, *Provincetown as a Stage: Provincetown, the Provincetown Players, and the Discovery of Eugene O'Neill* (1994), is what it says; for another, more personal look at the story, Agnes Boulton's *Part of a Long Story* (1958) has at its center the author's life with Eugene O'Neill in Provincetown. Karen Krahulik, *Provincetown: From Pilgrim Landing to Gay Resort* (2005), and Peter Manso, *Ptown: Art, Sex, and Money on the Outer Cape* (2002), are both worth reading.

The local histories mentioned above slant toward the seventeenth and eighteenth centuries. Henry Crocker Kittredge, *Shipmasters of Cape Cod* (1935), is the standard work on the age of sail; Admont Clark's *American Neptune* article, "They Built Clipper Ships in Their Back Yard" (1963; printed as a pamphlet 2001), chronicles the Shiverick Shipyard of Dennis; the standard work on the building of the Cape Cod Canal is William J. Reid, *The Building of the Cape Cod Canal, 1627–1914* (1961).

The best book on Cape Cod's creation as a resort is James C. O'Connell, *Becoming Cape Cod: Creating a Sea-Side Resort* (2002).

Cape Cod also has many museums, which are worth visiting and revisiting.

acknowledgments

THANKS TO WEBSTER BULL, for suggesting I undertake this book. My research assistant, Thomas Roland Brown, tirelessly found sources on the National Seashore and other topics; thanks to him, and to Dean Michael Shinagel and Suzanne Spreadbury of the Harvard Extension School for creating the research assistants program. Thanks to Amber Kopp at Suffolk University, who has also unearthed some rare photos.

The Boston Athenaeum has terrific collections on Cape Cod—special thanks to Stephen Nonack for suggesting books, Catharina Slautterback and Sally Pierce in the print department for finding images, and Mike Pagliaro for sharing thoughts on the Cape.

Lorna Condon at Historic New England showed me Cape-related treasures in their archives. Thanks also to Peter Stott at the Massachusetts Historical Commission; Aaron Schmidt at the Boston Public Library; Peter Drummey, Anne Bentley, Conrad Wright, Kim Nusco, and Elaine Grublin at the Massachusetts Historical Society; Laurie M. Deredita at the Shain Library at Connecticut College; Heather Lammers from the McNay Museum in San Antonio; Maria Batista and Michael Lapides from the New Bedford Whaling Museum; Stephanie Standish and Brian Whisenhut of the Swope Art Museum in Terre Haute.

On the Cape, the Provincetown Public Library and the Snow Library in Orleans are treasures. Stephen Borkowski, from the Provincetown Art Commission, has graciously provided images from the town's outstanding, irreplaceable collection. Napi Van Derek's art collection, parts of which are on exhibit at the Pilgrim Monument and at his restaurant, is worth a visit to the Cape to see.

Special thanks to the staffs—working for love and occasionally short pay—who maintain these collections so carefully, and so graciously have allowed access: Tamsen Cornell and Bonnie Snow at the Orleans Historical Society; Mary Ann Gray at the Chatham Historical Society; Hal Granger at the Cuttyhunk Historical Society; and especially Mary Sicchio, from both the Falmouth Historical Society and the William Brewster Nickerson Room at Cape Cod Community College.

Above all, family. My cousin Thomas G. Davies has supplied paintings from his own collection and shared his knowledge of art colonies and art. My wife, Phyllis, has taken me to the Cape, and our sons, John and Philip, have tramped with me through its woods and along its beaches and plied its waters. John has joined me on research expeditions to Orleans, Chatham, and Eastham. Finally, the two Cape Codders to whom the book is dedicated and for whom mere thanks seem hardly enough.

index

Page numbers in italics refer to illustrations. Material in the chronology (pages 110–19) is not included in the index.